The Ten Wise and Foolish Virgins

(Which group do you belong?)

By
E. J. Guobadia

Copyright © 2012 by E. J. Guobadia

The Ten Wise and Foolish Virgins (Which group do you belong)?
by E. J. Guobadia

Printed in the United States of America

ISBN 9781619040649

All rights reserved solely by the author. The author guarantees all contents are original and do not infringe upon the legal rights of any other person or work. No part of this book may be reproduced in any form without the permission of the author. The views expressed in this book are not necessarily those of the publisher.

Unless otherwise indicated, Bible quotations are taken from The New King James Version of the Bible. Copyright © 1982 by Thomas Nelson, Inc. Used by permission; and The King James Version of the Bible.

www.xulonpress.com

DEDICATION

I dedicate this book to my Heavenly Father - the greatest Dad in the universe and beyond. The very best any child could ever wish for.

To my Lord Yeshua - the very essence of my being and life.

To my precious Holy Spirit – my best and most faithful Friend.

I am most privileged to be born again of: the incorruptible seed of the word of God, the blood of redemption and the Lord's covenant and by the Holy Spirit of the living God.

I have the indwelling presence of the Holy Spirit, access through and to the blood of his covenant, the priceless gift of the living word of God and the grace to live it. For these, I am eternally grateful.

Contents

Chapter 1. The Parable 13

Chapter 2. The Word and Us 17

Chapter 3. The Stand of the Bride 26

Chapter 4. The State of the Heart 36

Chapter 5. Our Paths 44

Chapter 6. The Cross and the Blood 54

Chapter 7. The Spirit and the Word 63

Chapter 8. The Oil 72

Chapter 9. The Word and the Mind 83

Chapter 10. Our Enemy 91

Chapter 11. Our Choices 101

Chapter 12. Trusting the Lord 113

Chapter 13. Preparation 121

Chapter 14. Abiding in Love 130

The Ten Wise and Foolish Virgins (Which group do you belong)?

Chapter 15. Knowing Who We Are 138

Chapter 16. Staying Strong and Focused 145

Chapter 17. Those Who Sell 151

PURPOSE

I have been born out of time
And into time
For such a time as this.

I stepped out of the timeless realm
Into this time to establish my Father's will
Here on Earth as it is in Heaven

The time is now revealed
The time has now come
To take out of the timeless realm into this time

For this purpose I was created
For this purpose I was sent
For this purpose I was born

Upon this my gaze is now fixed
My heart is now set
And my walk is established

And so should you because
Of same, you were born
If you are of him and in him. !!!

By J.E.G (©2012)

Introduction

Ten Wise & Foolish virgins
(To which group do you belong?)

Matthew 24:24
For false Christ's and false prophets will rise and show great signs and wonders to deceive, if possible, even the **elect**. – This is already happening.

Matthew 24:22
…… unless those days were shortened, no flesh would be saved; but for the elect's sake those days will be shortened. – The days are being shortened, why does time fly by so quickly these days?

In the parable of the Tares and wheat, it reads
…So the servants of the owner came and said to him, 'Sir, did you not sow good seed in your field? How then does it have tares?' [28] He said to them, 'An enemy has done this.' The servants said to him, 'Do you want us then to go and gather them up?' [29] But he said, 'No, lest while you gather up the tares you also uproot the wheat with them. [30] Let both grow together until the harvest and at the time of harvest I will say to the reapers, *"First gather together **the tares** and bind them in bundles to burn them, but gather **the wheat** into my barn."* - The angels that gather are already at work.

The Ten Wise and Foolish Virgins (Which group do you belong)?

It is written "I will speak to you in parables...
Matt.13: 10-11
[10] And the disciples came and said to Him, "Why do you speak to them in parables?"
[11] He answered and said to them, "Because it has been *given to you to know* the mysteries of the kingdom of heaven, but to them it has not been given.

It is our responsibility to seek knowledge of the TRUTH of God's word and pray for revelation and understanding of it, ask for wisdom and the humility of heart to submit to it in total trust and surrender – that is *if we will be willing!* **Are you?**

Chapter 1

The Parable

Matt 25:1-13:
Then the kingdom of heaven shall be likened to ten virgins who took their lamps and went out to meet the bridegroom. Now five of them were wise [having knowledge and good judgement; wise to - aware of, especially so as to know how to act; wise up – become alert and aware, *Concise Oxford Dictionary*] and five were foolish [lacking good sense or judgement, *Concise Oxford Dictionary*]. Those who were foolish took their lamps and took no oil with them, but the wise took oil in their vessels with their lamps. But while the bridegroom was delayed, they all slumbered and slept. And at midnight a cry was heard: 'Behold, the bridegroom is coming; go out to meet him!' Then all those virgins arose and trimmed their lamps. And the foolish said to the wise, 'Give us some of your oil, for our lamps are going out.' But the wise answered, saying, 'No, lest there should not be enough for us and you; but go rather to those who sell, and buy for yourselves.' And while they went to buy, the bridegroom came, and those who were ready went in with him to the wedding; and the door was shut. Afterward the other virgins came also, saying, 'Lord, Lord, open to us!' But he answered and said, 'Assuredly, I say to you, I do not know you.' Watch therefore, for you know neither the day nor the hour in which the Son of Man is coming.

The ten virgins signify the body of Christ in righteousness-those who have been redeemed and purified by the blood of our Lord and Saviour Jesus Christ. The lamp represents the spirit of man. See Proverbs 20:27 and Matthew 5:14-16 below.

Prov. 20:27
The spirit of man is **the candle** of the LORD, searching all the inward parts of the belly.

Matt 5:14-16
Ye are **the light** of the world. A city that is set on a hill cannot be hid. Neither do men light a candle and put it under a bushel, but on a candlestick; and it gives light unto all that are in the house. Let **your light** [the fruits of the Spirit] so shine before men, that they may see your good works, and glorify your Father which is in heaven.

The spirit of man becomes ignited and illuminated when he accepts Christ into his life at Salvation by the Holy Spirit who is the Spirit of the Lord, causing the spirit of man to be re-born and bringing it alive to God. That recreated, ignited spirit becomes one of the Lord's lamps, alight to the world. In other words, Christ, who is the Light of the world, comes into our spirit man by his spirit when we accept his redemptive work at the cross on our behalf and confess him as our Saviour and Lord. He lights up our spirit man.

Second Samuel 22:29 declares, "You are my light, oh Lord; the Lord shall enlighten my darkness". Ephesians 5:8 tells us that we were once darkness, but now we are light in the Lord, and we are admonished to walk as children of light!

As John 1:4 puts it, "In Him was life and the life was the light of men." Further on in John 1, we have the following explanation:

And the light shines in the darkness, and the darkness did not comprehend it. There was a man sent from God, whose name was John. This man came for a witness, to bear witness of the Light that all through Him might believe. He was not that Light, but was sent to bear witness of that Light. That was

The Parable

the true Light which gives light to every man coming into the world. He was in the world, and the world was made through Him, and the world did not know Him. (John 1:5-10).

The light in this passage represents Jesus Christ our Lord. In addition to light, the word of God give us Spirit and life. "It is the Spirit who gives life; the flesh profits nothing. The words that I speak to you are Spirit, and they are life" (John 6:63).

We learn more about Spirit and light in Revelation 4:5. "And out of the throne proceeded lightning and thundering and voices: and there were seven <u>lamps</u> of fire burning before the throne, which are the seven <u>Spirits</u> of God. Christ said, "No one lights a Lamp and puts it under a Bushel"! In other words, the evidence that we are born again should begin to show through us from our spirit man.

Salvation is a walk in which the destination is an eternal abode with our Lord, either through death or through the "catching away," as many know it, but to meet with the Lord.

We will be living for eternity with the Bridegroom who is the head of the Church, of which we are members and parts of His body. That is, we have the right to live with Him after we have become born again and choose to walk in the light of His word and in obedience to his will! The bridegroom in this parable represents Christ Jesus.

Jesus tells us of the home he is building for us in John 14:1-3: "Let not your heart be troubled; you believe in God, believe also in me. In My Father's house are many mansions; if it were not so, I would have told you. I go to prepare a place for you. And if I go and prepare a place for you, I will come again and receive you to myself; that where I am, there you may be also."

I once read in a Bible commentary that no relevant importance should be attached to this parable of the ten virgins as it is just a parable. I however beg to differ because from the first time I read this parable in the Bible, it haunted me so to speak and I have often meditated on it until the Lord woke me up one night and told me to pick up a pen and a book and begin to write. I do not know how long I wrote, but I wrote enough to give birth to this book, and the Lord himself has also restrained me from publishing it until now. So I am convinced that it is a message for the Church at this hour.

Besides it is also written in the Bible that in parables He will speak to us. Psalm 78:1-2 says, "Give ear, Oh my people, to my law; incline your ears to the words of my mouth. I will open my mouth in a **parable**; I will utter things **kept secret** from the foundations of the world."

If we truly take time to study the Lord's parables and prayerfully seek their revelations and understanding, we will discover a lot of hidden messages in them, much more than we are already aware of. We are entitled to this knowledge because they are for us and will be revealed to us by His Holy Spirit, but we have to be willing to seek the true knowledge and revelation of His WORD!

When the disciples of Jesus asked why he spoke to people in parables, he answered and said, "Because it has been given to you to know the mysteries of heaven, but to them it has not been given" (Matt. 13:11).

Earlier in the scriptures, God told the prophet Daniel something similar. "And he said, 'Go your way, Daniel, for the words are closed up and sealed till the time of the end. Many shall be purified, made white, and refined, but the wicked shall do wickedly; and none of the wicked shall understand, but <u>the wise</u> shall understand. (Daniel 12:9-10)

Chapter 2

The Word and Us

"*N*ow five of them were wise and five were foolish" (Matthew 25:2). Half of the virgins were wise. In order words, they had the fear of the Lord hence they received their wisdom. How do I know these virgins feared the Lord? Proverbs 9:10 declares, "The fear of the Lord is the beginning of wisdom, and the knowledge of the Holy One is understanding."

The other half of the virgins, however, were foolish. In order words, they lacked wisdom or according to the Oxford dictionary, they lacked "good sense or judgment."

The fear of the Lord will cause us to pursue righteousness by abiding continually in Him and in His word. By seeking what His will is and following in that path. Even in the areas where we find it hard to surrender to His will because of self and flesh, God will assist us. If we cry out to him, He will help us because we are promised in His word that, "for it is God who works in you both to will and to do for *His* good pleasure". (Philippians 2:13).

The problem so many of us have is that we want to serve God, but we are not willing to die to self and flesh (soul and body) in a lot of areas because it is not convenient for us to do so. It disrupts our comfort zones and destroys our justifications for doing the things we do that are gratifying to our carnal nature, which we feel are ours by right, and we are not ready to give those up because they are pleasing to our flesh.

So many of us are also too earthly bound that we are hardly heavenly conscious, except when we are in spiritual environments! On the flip side of that, we must not be so heavenly bound that we are no earthly good either. We must be balanced! We are to be the light of the world and not of heaven, because there is no darkness in heaven. We are also to be the salt of the earth, as it is decaying and needs something to help preserve it. There is no decay in heaven!

Too many of us live out of the realm of our emotions, rather than in the knowledge of, and in submission to the word of God! The enemy takes great pleasure in attacking our emotions through unrenewed minds. One of the quickest ways to grow spiritually is to deliberately, willingly and continuously submit our emotions to the word and will of God. That is, rather than respond to people or situations out of our emotions or feelings, we deliberately choose to respond according to the word or will of God! Hence, it is important for us to know the word! The Psalmist says, "Your word have *I hidden in my heart* that *I might not* sin against you" (Ps 119:11).

Our heart is the seat of our emotions and whatever we allow to dwell in it is bound to spill over into other areas of our lives; hence, the Bible says to guard it with *"all diligence, for out of it flows the issues of life!"* (Prov. 4:23). If we do not learn and practice to deliberately and consciously hide the word of God in our hearts through mediating upon them and submitting our will to obey them, then the enemy will fill it for us through our minds with his thoughts, even when we are Christians with new hearts!

Peter said to Sapphira and Ananias in Acts 5:3, ". Why has Satan *filled* your heart to lie to the Holy Spirit?" If we refuse to guard our hearts with *all diligence* (careful and persistent work or effort) and fail to **hide the word of God in our hearts,** then we give ground and room for the enemy to fill it for us with his motives and intentions, most especially when we are not yet dead to old ungodly habits and we act these out consciously and unconsciously without proper processing. The Lord himself taught in the Bible that defilement comes from within. "It is not what goes into the mouth that defiles a man; but what comes out of the mouth, this defiles a man" (Matt 25:8). In other words, what comes out of his heart! It is from the abundance of the heart that the mouth speaks, according to the Bible.

Proverbs 23:7 says, "as a man thinks in his heart, so is he". In other words, a man displays in his character the true state of his heart.

Prov. 27: 19 says that the heart of a man **reveals** him. So whatever we permit, or allow to dwell in our hearts, that is what we will manifest! We have to know what has been written in the word of God, let it take hold of our mind through constant meditation and learn to hide it in our hearts. Then, we will be able to manifest it through the power of the Holy Spirit that dwells in us.

The word of God is powerful. Hebrews 4:12 says, "For the word of God is living and powerful, and sharper than any two edged sword piercing even to the division of soul and spirit and joints and marrow and is a **discerner of the thoughts** and **intents** of the heart" (bold is mine).

The word of God in us will discern - i.e. recognize or find out that which is of God or of our flesh, and will help us to know the difference between that and what is from the enemy. When we have the word in us, it will also rise up in our defence!

When the enemy attacked Jesus, He responded by repeating what was written and quoted the written word faithfully, showing us exactly how we are also to respond to the enemy when he attacks or invades our minds with thoughts that will lead us into sin, or into acting contrary to God's will and commandments.

Wisdom declares in the book of Proverbs, 8: 32-35, "Now therefore listen to me my children, for blessed are those who keep my ways [obedience]. Hear instructions and be wise and do not disdain it [Pay attention to the word of God and let it be dear to you; don't take it lightly]. Blessed is the man who listens to me, watching daily at my gates [paying attention to, and abiding in, the word daily], waiting at the post of my doors [meditating upon the word]. For whoever finds me finds life [whoever resolves in their heart to abide in, yield to, and obey the word of a God] and obtain favour from the Lord."

The Bible also tells us that he who sins against the word of God WRONGS his own soul. The soul that sins shall die! (Ezekiel 18:4). That is, the soul that chooses to continue in sin, knowing that he has been redeemed by the precious blood of the lamb, will surely die if they do not repent and turn away from sin.

Psalm 19:7 tell us that "the law of the Lord is perfect, *converting* the soul; the testimony of the Lord is sure *making wise* the simple." But those who are not converted by the law of the Lord will suffer the consequences.

As Proverbs 8:36 puts it, "and those who hate me [those who hate the knowledge of the truth of God's word] love death!"

Proverbs 19:2 tells us that "it is not good for a soul to be without knowledge." The word of the Lord further declares that "*my people* perish for lack of knowledge" (Hosea 4:6). (Italics mine) *not the world, but God's people.* That is, God's people lack the true knowledge and revelation of the word of God, and even of the world in which they live!

We need the true knowledge of God's word to fully understand and know who we really are as children of God and to understand our purpose and duty here on earth. When we fully understand this, we will come to understand why, though we are in the world, we are not of the world. When we come to the true understanding of this, we will become more focused on our God-given purpose on earth and will be more determined to fulfil it at all costs!

Too many people are suffering from what I call an identity crisis. Unfortunately, even Christians suffer from this too. We are aware that we are now of Christ, yet not many of us have the true revelation and understanding of what this truly means even though we confess it. In (Dan. 11:32), the Bible says those who *know* their God shall be strong and *do* great exploits - (Italics mine). How much and how well do we really know him, even though we have been born again for a while now-myself included. I believe and know that the more we seek God and do not become weary, the more He will reveal Himself to us. I also believe that the more we truly seek God through Christ Jesus who is the word of God, the more of ourselves we come to see and know. I am convinced that a man cannot truly know himself until he knows God deeply. Then he will come to understand who he truly is. We can only know God through Christ, who has come to reveal Him through His word and his Holy Spirit and we cannot have the Holy Spirit until we are born again. The carnal mind - i.e., the natural man cannot understand the things of God because they are spiritually discerned. (1st Corinthians 2:14). In other words, it takes a spiritually re-born and ignited spirit of man to understand the things of the Spirit of God.

In Matt 24:4, it says, "And Jesus answered and said to them, 'Take heed that no one deceives you'" How would we know whether we are being deceived or not if we are not grounded in the word of God through the knowledge, revelation and understanding of it?

So I have since come to the conclusion that the only way a man can truly know himself, who he really is, why he was created, the purpose for which he was sent into the world and how to accomplish it- is by knowing the God who created him and sent him forth. You know Him through His word and reverent fellowship with Him in constant communion. You can only know God by knowing who Christ is because He is the only one who has come down to reveal God to us and sealed up that knowledge with His blood to be acknowledged by the world and revealed to those who come to him.

By the way, anyone is welcome. As it is written, "whosoever calls upon the name of the Lord shall be saved" (Acts 2:21). That is, when a man calls upon the Lord by faith believing in who He is and his ability to deliver him. When he confesses him as Lord, then that man (or woman) will receive the gift of eternal salvation.

When we are saved by being born again- ("Except a man be born again, he cannot see the kingdom of God"[John 3:3]), the mysteries of the kingdom of God can be revealed to us and can be seen by those that are his by his Holy Spirit. You cannot have the Holy Spirit and his indwelling power outside of Christ! In the days of old, God gave His Spirit to the prophets to fulfil His purpose for whatever He called them to do. Now, however, we get it only through Christ, as He has declared, "All power in heaven and on earth has been given to me" (Matt. 28:18).

It is written, "But as many as received him, to them, he gave the right or authority to become children of God, to those who believe in his name; who were born, not of blood, nor of the will of the flesh, but of God" (John1:12-13). The Lord blessed the creation of his hand. Even if a man has more than he knows what to do with, without being born again, he may not truly fulfil his spiritual destiny and calling. If his spiritual destiny or journey is not fulfilled, he has not truly fulfilled his purpose in life and you can only truly know your spiritual destiny through being in Christ. When a man comes to know and understand his God-given destiny and gifts, he will not need to go through life surviving and living from pay check to pay check. He will not fear the loss of a job or recession because he would have come to understand his true source. He would come to know his gift and continue to reproduce himself, and his true source will never run dry. Even if there are others with the same type of gifting, there will be something unique about his particular gift. God has enough time to give each one of us a unique fingerprint and number the individual hair on our heads. I don't know how many strands of hair I have on my head, and I have never met anyone else who knows, but the Lord knows because he numbered them.

Mathew 10:28 states "And do not fear those who kill the body but cannot kill the soul. But rather fear Him who is able to destroy both soul and body in hell. [29] Are not two sparrows sold for a copper coin? And not one of them falls to the ground apart from your Father's will. [30] ***But the very hairs of your head are all numbered.***(Italics and bold mine)

The gifts that the Lord gives a man to live by and bless the world with will keep making room for him, and he will continue to stand before great men and kings if he chooses to be diligent with it, as there will always be demand for his gifts. If the world doesn't need it, the Lord won't give it! He does not believe in waste. The gift will enable the man to keep reproducing, or reinventing, himself. It will just flow out naturally and effortlessly because the God-given source of it is on the inside of him, and he will not live life tolerating his existence.

God told Joshua, in the book of Deuteronomy, chapter one, verse eight, "this book of the law shall not depart from your mouth [let it be your confession always], but you *shall meditate* in it day and night, that *you may observe to do according to all that is written in it. For then you will make your way prosperous and then you will have good success.*"(Italics and bold mine).

Reading the word of God out of religious duty is not enough! That gives us head knowledge. We *must meditate* on it day and night, according to God's word, for it is in meditation that revelation comes. Revelation will give us a deeper, and better, understanding of the word of God. Understanding will give us good and sound knowledge of the word, and that will give us wisdom. Wisdom will teach us the fear of the lord. The fear of the lord will cause us to walk in humility and OBEDIENCE to God's word. Obedience will cause us to walk in LOVE towards the Father and mankind, and that is what conquers all, for God is love, and we are to manifest Him here on earth by allowing His light to shine through us!

We have to know what has been written in the word of God- let it take hold of our minds and learn to hide it in our hearts by submitting our will to obey it in obedience to God.

The word of God is a testament that has been sealed with the blood of His everlasting covenant, and no power in Hell can stop its working power except us. When, as Christians, we refuse to abide in it as we ought, when we won't declare it and stand on it because of doubt and fear, thereby not speaking in agreement with God's word, but taking thoughts from the enemy and saying with our mouths what the enemy throws into our minds as fiery darts, when we knowingly disobey the truth of the word of God that we know, we violate the abiding power of His blood covenant and the protecting power of His testament that is a covering over us. In other words, we create unnecessary doorways for the enemy into our lives. It is written, "whoever breaks the hedge [i.e., the hedge of divine protection around us], the serpent will bite".

So often in our lives, when we choose to disobey God's word, we become contaminated by the poison of the serpent, and we think that because we have disobeyed God's word and repented of it, it is over, not realising that we have simply sown and will certainly reap! For as long as the Earth remains, seed-time and harvest shall not cease (Genesis 8:22). Several verses speak of this truth. For example, "God cannot be mocked, whatever a man sows, he shall also reap!" (Gal. 6:7). When we repent and ask God for forgiveness, he certainly does forgive, and it is wiped out of the record book of Heaven, as the Lord remembers it no more. However because we have sown it here on earth, we still reap its harvest! Whatever you sow on the Earth, the Earth reproduces for you sooner or later. David genuinely repented of his sins before God, and God forgave him and even blessed him with another child who became a king, but that did not stop David from reaping the harvest of what he did! Some might say God overlooks what is done in ignorance. That is certainly true because, what you do not understand as sin, the Lord will not judge you by. Paul said, in Romans 7:7, "...I would not have known sin except through the law. For I would not have known covetousness unless the Lord had said 'thou shall not covet'." However, when we come to understand sin as sin and yet deliberately and knowingly commit it with the intention of repenting later (I used to do it in times past when I was not a growing Christian and have also heard some Christians say that they did that, as well), there is no excuse for that. When I go through some stuff with people, I ask myself this – Am I reaping, or are they sowing?

Some of us go through life knowingly (as we refuse to die to self and submit to God's word) breaking the hedge and repenting, thereby remaining in a continuous circle of failures and stagnation, and then we question why things are not working for us. My question is: What are we doing with the truth of the word of God that we know? The ones we do not know, how eager and determined are we to know them so we will truly be free? As it is written, "you shall know the truth and the truth will **make you free**" (John. 8:32). True freedom for us as Christians here on earth comes from abiding within the restrictive freedom of the word of God, the blood of Christ, and the leading presence of the Holy Spirit.

1 Peter1:2 states we are elect unto OBEDIENCE and sprinkling of the BLOOD OF CHRIST! The obedience comes first, before the sprinkling of the blood. We are also told to submit ourselves to God, resist the enemy, and then he will flee from us! The submitting to God's word and will comes first, before we attempt to resist the enemy and then he has no choice but to flee from us according the word of God.

So you see, we cannot wilfully continue to live in disobedience to God's word and expect the blood to effectively work for us! If Rahab had not **obeyed** by tying the scarlet cord, which represented the blood line, she and her household would have been killed. If the children of Israel had not **obeyed** by staying within and under the blood covering and had come out, they would have died along with the Egyptians. Next time, before we go wielding the blood of Christ, let's examine our walk of obedience. I am not talking here about when we stumble and miss the mark. We should be quick to repent. I am talking about a life of <u>continuous and wilful disobedience,</u> despite knowing the truth of the word of God concerning whatever it is we are doing. We cannot claim our rights in the victorious power of the blood of Christ and at the same time, not walk in honour and reverence of what the blood has done for us or walk in honour of the word of the same Christ and His Spirit! It is written that there are three that bear witness on earth - the Spirit, the water, (which is the word) and the blood, and these three agree as one (1 John. 5:7).

Later on in the book of First John (5:18), it is written, "We know that whoever is born of God does not sin; but he who has been born of God keeps himself, and the wicked one does not touch him". The Lord said "the evil one came and found nothing in me" (John 14:30).

Our obedience to God's word does not increase God in any shape or form, nor does it decrease Him. It is for our own good, wellbeing, and safe keeping!

Chapter 3

The Stand of the Bride

*I*n the book of Ephesians, chapter five, verses 25-27, it is written, "Husbands love your wives just as Christ also loves the Church and gave himself for her, that he might sanctify and cleanse her with the washing of water by the word, that he might present her to himself a glorious Church not having spot or wrinkle or any such thing, but that she should be holy and without blemish!" We, as the bride of Christ that he laid down his life for, have now been set apart, and we NEED to continuously allow ourselves to get washed by the word of God and submit to it because that is what will keep us spotless here now and at his coming. Jesus prayed to the Father in John 17:17, "Sanctify [set apart] them [the church] by your Truth. Your word is truth."

Can you imagine a Bride that has been set apart (redeemed by the blood) and dressed up (with a robe of righteousness because of the blood) for her groom, playing around with pools of muddy water? In this case, we are talking about sin. Every bride in the natural is very particular about how they look in their bridal gown (our robe of righteousness), and they are aware that they will be the centre of attention, so they are very conscious of how they present themselves to the guests, bystanders, and especially the groom. There is no way you will not notice who the bride is because she will definitely stand apart, or stand out, because of her dressing and also because

The Stand Of The Bride

of the way she will carry herself. The guests and bystanders are the world, and they should notice that we are the Bride of Christ, even if some of them don't know or understand who Christ is! They should notice us by our dress (robe of righteousness) and by the way we carry ourselves (our way of life)!

When we now choose to play around with pools of muddy water (that's exactly what we do when we yield to sin and walk in disobedience to His word and will for our lives) and have our garments all muddy and soiled, even when we as the Church try to tell the world we are the Bride, they acknowledge what we say, but they don't take us seriously. Why should they, when we don't look like we are a REAL BRIDE? A real bride doesn't need to announce it. People automatically know who she is because it will be obvious. For some of us, our garments don't look much different from the worlds. A real bride in the natural has enough common sense to know to avoid muddy pools of water like the plague because she doesn't want her garment stained with anything at all. She is very particular about presenting herself spotless - both to the world and to her groom!

The book of Revelation says, "behold I am coming as a thief; blessed is he who watches and keeps his garments [garment of righteousness], lest he walk naked and they see his shame" (16:15). The Lord also told the dead church of Sardis in Revelation 3:4 that they have a few people among them who still have not defiled their garments, and they shall walk with him in white for they are worthy.

1 Peter 2:2 states, "As newborn babes, desire the pure milk of the word that you may grow thereby". I believe it is also safe to interpret this as: as new born again Christians, desire and acquire the pure oil of the word in your mind, and choose in your hearts to obey it to keep your lamp burning because you are the light of the world.

Exodus 27:20 says, "And you shall command the children of Israel that they bring you **pure oil** of pressed olive for the light to **cause** the **lamp to burn continually** (underline and bold mine)". I am confident that the Lord will get us there, for those who are willing to be cleansed and those who will go the extra mile to acquire extra oil!

The Ten Wise and Foolish Virgins (Which group do you belong)?

Proverbs 30:5 says every word of God is PURE. He is a shield to those who put their trust in him. There are so many Christians who are born again, spirit-filled, yet very spiritually immature. This group included me until a short while back (I am just now beginning to grow). These Christians stay immature because they have simply refused to grow! I am amazed to have even come across pastors and ministers who fit this description and I often wonder exactly what they are sharing with their flocks. I am especially concerned about some of those that shoot out of Bible school and set up their own churches, not ready to serve so that character may be built.

If that is what the Lord has specifically commanded for an individual, there is nothing wrong with it. If the one that shoots out from Bible school to the pulpit is willing to humble himself to grow as he goes along, there is nothing wrong with that either. However, I am talking about the ones that can't wait to be their own bosses with a level of anointing and whichever spiritual gift they have manifesting. Some of us also have a way of putting our pastors and ministers on a pedestal that we create for them and put bars of idolization around them that cage them into a position where they now find it difficult to reveal any area of vulnerability that they may have and might need some help with! So they are forced to put up a front that conforms to what is expected of a Pastor or Minister. I have especially observed this in African church circles. I have come across leaders, so to speak, who try to control, manipulate and intimidate their flock into submitting to their will, and it is so sad to see that. Such church leaders need to deal with issues of insecurity and inferiority in their own lives before they are able to help others. We all need help from the Lord. The needs may vary, but we will always need His help!

Let me make it absolutely clear that this is not an attack on leaders. God forbid that I would dishonour His servants, but there are some truths that need to be told in order that we might be able to check and judge ourselves so that we won't come under God's judgement. We all as Christians ought to be in a place of trust with one another - a place where we are not afraid for our brothers and sisters to see our vulnerability for fear of them taking advantage of us. We need them to pray with and stand by us. I am convinced that this is why some of us fall, including ministers, and they fall harder than most. When they do, we turn against them and persecute them instead of standing in the gap for them and crying out to the Lord to see them through it. The leadership position can sometimes be quite lonesome, but for the Spirit of the Lord. I do know however that the Lord will get us where we need to be if we will be willing to walk with and submit to Him. He will never override any man's will.

James 1:21 tells us to lay aside all filthiness and overflow of wickedness and receive with meekness the implanted word of God which is able to save your souls. The Bible says "the soul that sins shall die." Our souls need to be cleansed and purified by the word of God so that they will come into alignment with the sanctification that the Lord has already established for us through the redemption of our minds! Hence it is written that "we have the mind of Christ!" We have to have our mind which is a part of our soul, renewed by the word of God to such an extent that it comes in alignment, agreement and submission to our spirit man, controlled by the Holy Spirit!

If we do not constantly renew our minds with, and habitually meditate upon the word of God, we will have a very difficult, miserable and unfulfilling Christian walk. It will not be the devil's fault, but ours. There is absolutely nothing that the enemy can do with the word of God except to **tempt** you to doubt it and *the choice will be yours* to agree to doubt the word or to confess it faithfully, as Christ did. To stand confidently on it, irrespective of what the surrounding circumstances are.

When Peter asked the Lord to command him to walk on water and the Lord did, Peter began to walk on water at the keeping power of the word that the Lord spoke until he took his focus off Christ, who is the word. Then Peter began to sink and cried out to the Lord to save him. The Lord asked, "Why *did you* doubt?" The enemy stirred up the distractions around Peter, just as he still does with the saints today. The Lord did not blame nor rebuke the storm on this occasion. Rather, he asked Peter why he doubted. In other words, "Why did you agree with, and accept what you saw despite my command (word) that empowered you to be able to walk on water in the first place? Why did you choose to doubt and not believe that the word I spoke that started and enabled you to walk on water in the first place would keep you? Remember Hebrews 12:2, "He is the author and finisher of our faith". Also notice that the storm ceased as soon as the Lord took hold of Peter, and they both stepped back into the boat (Matt. 14:22-33).

I remember a period when I was meditating on the scripture that defines faith, Hebrews 11:1, which says, "Now faith is the substance of things hoped for, the evidence of things not seen." I kept repeating it to myself, trying so hard to fully understand it in my mind. Out of the blue, I heard the Holy Spirit say, "Let me make it simple for you – faith is CONFIDENT BELIEF AND RIGID EXPECTATION!" So I analysed each word, one by one, and understood the verse perfectly!

The Bible says we are the light of the world and the salt of the earth. The world is a dark place and, even as we speak, it's getting darker, but it does not matter how deep the darkness is, it can never cover LIGHT! Salt preserves. The world is corrupt and getting worse by the day, and we are to be the preserving agents for God.

I recently saw in a vision, so much darkness everywhere, but at the same time, I saw that even in the midst of the darkness, there were people who were moving about easily from place to place while others were very fearful and looking confused, not sure of where to turn, where to go, or who to trust. The people who were moving about easily from place to place had shafts of light like huge torches from heaven on them, and everywhere they went, they moved with ease, gladness of heart and they never stumbled. I heard the Lord say, "those are the obedient Christians". Psalm 119:165 says, "Great peace have those who love your law [the word], and nothing causes them to stumble."

I used to think that being obedient was a very difficult task to accomplish, not understanding anything about how to yield to the Holy Spirit, the flesh or how to die to it. I also used to think about what Christ said about his yoke being easy and his burden light, and I began to ponder that there must be a way.

When I became born again, no one really told me the importance of studying the word of God, let alone how to meditate on it and yield to it. Much later, when I began to read the Bible and other books, I began to understand these things myself. What I heard much of was how to give and receive, name it and claim it, deliverance and warfare. So I just kept giving and expecting to receive, but I did not really receive much and began to wonder why until one day when I heard very clearly an audible voice in my right ear saying, "seek first the kingdom of God and his righteousness, and all these things shall be added to you" (Matt.6:33). The word **righteousness** was gently, but emphatically stressed and I remembered that I had heard the scripture before, but I had not really taken time to understand it, so I began to ponder it.

Prior to this time, I was rebuking the devil so much, binding whatever I did not want and losing everything I wanted, whether it was of God or my flesh! What I did not realise was that my flesh needed much of the rebuking and binding that I was directing toward the devil! When we come into the kingdom, so many of us just want our problems gone without really being prepared to start dying to self, and that becomes our focus. Very rarely do we pursue the fear of God or his righteousness. In fact, most of us just want God to keep blessing us on top of the way we are and, when it comes to dying to self, we begin to rebel and are not as willing to do that as we are to receive the blessings of God. In other words, we eagerly start to seek the other things that are meant to be added for free and expect His righteousness to somehow tag along and allow it to manifest itself at our convenience.

Then I came across the book of Romans and started to read the rest of the Epistles, and I began to understand what Amos 3:6 says about agreeing with the Lord and walking with Him. To walk in total surrender to Him means total death to self, which takes a process of abiding in the word, letting the word abide in you, surrendering to it, and obeying it in humility and in love.

We, as humans, expect our children to grow up and start taking responsibilities that will prepare them to become responsible adults in society and contribute well to it. God as well, expects us His children, to grow up in Christ and start taking responsibilities in preparation for the purpose for which He has created and sent us into the world. The Bible says we are the light of the world and the salt of the earth which is true, but manifesting it requires transforming our minds by renewing them with the word of God, presenting our bodies as living sacrifices unto God, and walking in the Spirit so that we will not fulfil the lust of the flesh. We walk in the spirit by living and walking in the word.

Not long after I was born again, I found myself in some very difficult situations and the only thing I knew to do was to fast and pray. However, because I was not really sure how to pray about the problems, I started to cry before God and the only words I knew were "call upon me, and I will answer you", "seek and you will find", "knock and it shall be opened unto you," and those words were what I kept repeating. I became so grieved and troubled that I started to cry out loud to God, reminding Him of these words, and I kept saying over and over, "Lord, you promised" while stamping my foot on the floor. I was seriously bowling, as I felt like I was between the soldiers of Egypt and the Red Sea. I had started crying at about 11 am and I was not willing to stop until the Lord answered me.

'Round about 2:00 to 2:15 p.m., I suddenly heard a voice behind me saying, "What do you want?", but because I knew that I was all alone in the room, I decided it must be my imagination and I just carried on crying without turning. After a few moments, I heard again and more emphatically this time and somewhat impatiently, the same voice and the same question. I spun around to see a huge Angel standing in front of the wardrobe near the door to the room, and I was stunned! He was about eight or more feet tall, with long shoulder-length blond hair, piercing blue eyes, and features that looked like they were chiselled out of marble. He had huge, sparkling white and very fluffy-looking wings, and he stood with his feet slightly apart, his arms folded across his chest. He wore a sparkling white gown with one gold coloured silk cord around his mid rib. I just stared at him, wide-eyed, with my mouth hanging open.

The silence was broken when he asked me a third time, "What do you want"?

That startled me out of my shock, and I quickly thought about all the family problems on my shoulder (being the eldest in my family, with my father dead, I had a lot of responsibilities on me). I had taken the place of a father from a young age of seventeen, and it was a tremendous responsibility for a teenage girl to carry single handed. I sensed the angel was in a hurry, and I thought to myself that he did not look like he had the time to wait for me to analyse all the problems, one after the other, so I just blurted out, "I NEED A MIRACLE. Before 6 p.m. today, I need a miracle," as I was totally fed up with the situations. As soon as I said that, he lifted himself off the floor and disappeared through the roof.

I sat rooted there for a few seconds, and then I fled the room myself. As I was running through the passage to look for my junior brother who was in another part of the house to tell him what had just happened, I remembered another young man of God who was a pastor and used to tell me about seeing Angels and visions. I was not yet born again then and as such, I did not believe a word he said. I knew he used to fast and pray a lot, and I just concluded that he must be hallucinating from abstaining from food for long periods of time. I was however, too polite to tell him so. Whenever he visited our home (he is my brother's friend) and left, I used to laugh at him behind his back and always told my brother to advise his friend to go eat some food so that he would stop seeing things, as I was seriously convinced that too much fasting was causing him to hallucinate. All of a sudden, it hit me - after what had just happened to me, that he must have been telling me the truth about seeing Angels, and I fell to my knees right in the hallway and began to ask the Lord to forgive me for all my mockery of this young pastor. After that, I got up to continue looking for my brother to tell him about what I had just seen.

At exactly 5:45 p.m. that same day, I got a miracle. Other small miracles and experiences had happened during the course of the day that finally led me to where I got the biggest miracle that I really needed. The funny thing was that, because I was

The Ten Wise and Foolish Virgins (Which group do you belong)?

so caught up in the activities surrounding me at that moment, I had forgotten about the Angel visitation earlier that day. As I was leaving where I was with such joy and gladness in my heart at having received what I had been praying about for a long time, I heard very quietly in my right ear, "it's not yet six o'clock, and you have your miracle," and it hit me all at once again - the Angel visitation that afternoon, my request about needing a miracle before 6 p.m., and the fact that I had just received the most important miracle of all that I needed right then. I froze, and I was not sure whether to jump so high and hit my head on the roof for joy or to simply slump to the ground and weep for joy. I was simply overwhelmed with emotion at the faithfulness of the Father at the cry of one of his children. Truly, the Lord is faithful.

The other part of this experience, however, was that, about six years after this experience, I was in another country and going through some hard times again. So, after a while, I told my friend that I was going to cry unto the Lord again as I had shared this experience with her previously. I asked her to babysit my four-month-old daughter for me so that I could concentrate and would not be distracted with having to attend to the baby. My friend readily agreed and told me her own prayer needs as well. I went to a room upstairs in the house and sat on the floor and started to cry unto God, analysing all my problems. I believed that, since I had done the same thing before and He sent me an Angel and miracles followed after, that the same thing would also happen this time.

I started crying out at about 11 a.m. this time as well. Sometimes I would forget that I was praying and get carried away by other thoughts, and then I would suddenly remember that I was supposed to be at prayer and should concentrate, so I would resume praying again. I had been doing this for a while and, after about two hours or so, the mercy of God came and I heard, "What are you doing there?" I recognized the voice of the Lord straight away, and I replied, "Where?" The Lord repeated the same question, and this time I said, "I am crying". He said, "Crying for what?" I replied that I was crying for Him to send me an Angel like He did before. To my shock, He said in a matter-of-fact tone, "No angel is coming." I replied, in shock, "Why not?" And he said, "Grow up. You have my word, my Spirit, and my authority, so grow up. I sent you an Angel before because you were a baby in me and didn't know much except to cry, and I responded to your faith. Now you have been in me for some time and need to grow. You have my word, my Spirit, and the authority I gave you. Use it, and grow up".

I sat there in stunned silence, feeling very sheepish. After a while, I slowly stood up and went back down stairs where my friend was eagerly waiting, and she asked me, wide-eyed, "What happened? Has the Angel come?" I slowly shook my head with my mouth pouting, feeling very deflated and foolish. She was very curious to know what happened, and I told her what the Lord had said. Both of us started to discuss it, and I finally remembered a book I had previously come across titled *The Authority of the Believer* by Kenneth Hagin. I decided to buy it, as I was told it teaches about our authority as believers and I also made up my mind to start studying the word.

Rom 8:18-19 says, "For I consider that the sufferings of this present time are not worthy to be compared with the glory which shall be revealed in us, for the earnest expectation of the creation eagerly waits for the revealing of the sons of God."

Babies cannot be entrusted with power, neither do they go into battles, full-grown sons do! Therefore, we need to grow up! WE NEED TO GROW UP! THE LORD EXPECTS US TO!

Chapter 4

The State of the Heart

The Bible says, in Psalm 119:165, that, "great peace have those who love your law and nothing causes them to stumble." When we have the word of God in us and submit to it, we will not stumble!

Every Christian will automatically respond "yes" to the question, "Do you love the Lord?," but the true test of our loving him is found in John 14:21, "He who has my commandments and keeps them, [believes in, submits to, and OBEYS them], it is he who loves me, and he who loves me will be loved by my father, and I will love him and manifest [reveal] myself to him."

So before we answer "yes" to the question next time, we should pause and ask ourselves how much we really do obey Him (the Word). If we are in the habit of being quick to yield to our flesh instead of making a deliberate, conscious effort to yield to the word and the Spirit of God, then we deceive ourselves.

The Lord told us in Matthew 7:21-27, "Not everyone who says to me 'Lord, Lord' shall enter the kingdom of Heaven, but he who does the will [i.e., acts in obedience to His word; His word is His will] of my Father in heaven. Many will say to me in that day, 'Lord, Lord have we not prophesied in your name, cast out demons in your name and done many wonders in your name?' And then I will declare to them, 'I never knew you, depart from me you who practice lawlessness [i.e., you who continued to practice sin, despite knowing it was sin]'".

For you to be able to prophesy in the Lord's name, cast out demons in His name, and do many wonders in His name, it means you must have the authority of His name to do them. You have to have the gift of faith in His name, the backing power of the Holy Spirit to manifest them, and you can't have these without being born again! Even the prophets of old, who were not born again and still did miracles, knew God and were zealous for His name. They heard directly from God and spoke in faith, and the manifesting power of the Holy Spirit brought those things to come to pass. Yet, according to the Lord in the book of Mathew, he will tell them "I never knew you, depart from me you who practice lawlessness." In other words, I don't know you who continued in sin despite knowing it was sin."

You see, it is not how many miracles we perform or how popular we are as God's people or ministers on earth. It is how much we honour Him in our hearts with a life of obedience!

Verse 24 continues, "…therefore whoever hears these sayings of mine and does them [obeys], I will liken him to a wise man who built his house upon the rock [i.e., Christ who is our rock and the word of God combined], and the rains descended and the floods came and the winds blew [tests, trials and temptations] and beat on that house [us, as His temple], and it did not fall, for it was founded on the rock. But everyone who hears these sayings of mine and does not do them will be like a foolish man who built his house upon the sand [dust- Man was made from dust; hence, he is flesh apart from the Spirit of the Lord that comes to perfect him at redemption], and the rain descended, the floods came and the winds blew and beat on that house; and it fell, and great was its fall." In other words, this man's entire life was built on living in the flesh and not in the Word nor in the Spirit of the Lord that had been freely given to him! (Words in brackets, mine).

The Lord told me not too long ago, just as He turned to leave after talking to me about the end time and the state of the Church, "One more thing," and I said, "Yes, Lord." He said, "Obey my word not because you are afraid of going to hell but because you love me." He paused and looked deeply at me, and then said very quietly, "In that, I am honoured."

When he told me that, something happened on the inside of me that I cannot exactly put into words to this day, save to say that I am now desperate above all else to love Him with the greatest passion in me and obey Him all the way whether my flesh feels like it or not, whether it makes sense to me or not, whether my emotions like it or not! When He looked deeply at me and said those words, every carnal rebellion in me just seemed to shrivel and melt away. Conviction became overwhelmingly strong, and I saw my selfishness. Truly, the carnal mind is at enmity (Rom.8:7) with God if you allow it to rule, even though you are a Christian. As long as we allow ourselves to be ruled by our carnal mind, which is the mind of our flesh rather than the mind of our newly recreated spirit filled with the word of God, we will never truly live a life of obedience to God!

When I was eight years old, something happened to me, and I was in heaven for a few hours. On the 9th of April 1996, between 2:00 and 3 p.m., I was caught up in the Spirit twice to see Hell and its location. It is in the belly of the earth and has the shape of a human figure, sprawled out on its back with arms and legs spread apart. It looked like it was hewn out of very hard, unbreakable rock. Since then, I have become very conscious of not wanting to end up in hell, having seen the difference between the two places. So, the truth of the matter is, I've often obeyed the word of God more out of the fear of not wanting to end up in hell rather than out of reverential fear and love for God. I understood exactly why the Lord said what He said. Not that I do not love Him, but I have clearly not loved Him enough to often obey Him out of pure, submissive love when my flesh was screaming to go in the opposite direction, especially when I felt justified in my actions. The word of God says, however, that He is the One who justifies! Oftentimes, we do things without realising what we are doing because the human nature is basically selfish and will justify its actions while judging another's.

The word of God says, in Romans 2:21, "You who teach another, do you teach yourself? You who preach that a man should not steal, do you steal?" I remember, after having been some time in a church that loved God dearly, but also had a spirit of religion unknown to them, I visited another fast growing church in the area and concluded that there was too much worldliness there and in the people. This self-made opinion stayed with me concerning this particular church.

I love shoes. I and my siblings inherited this love for shoes from my late Dad. So I do buy shoes often especially the ones with matching bags. Over the years, I had come to acquire a lot of shoes.

I also often give away shoes, both old and new. Even friends and family often consult me when they have special occasions to celebrate and need to buy shoes because they say I have great taste when it comes to buying shoes. Sometimes I even buy shoes that are neither my size nor my children's, but just because they're really beautiful and have a unique design that I love, hoping to meet someone to whom I can give the shoes to as a gift! It's that crazy.

So, one day as I sat watching the Christian channel on television, this church came on and the thought 'this worldly church' came into my mind because this had become the subconscious opinion that I carried for this particular church. I got up shortly after that and went up to my bedroom. As you step into my bedroom, the first thing that hits you is the array of shoes in clear plastic shoe boxes from near the ceiling to the floor. All over my room are shoes and most of them new and unworn, despite the fact that I have been buying them for a while. I am not the outgoing or party type, so I do not really need that many shoes. I just really like to look at them and buy them. Once I even bought eight different colours in one particular design of shoe and bag set because I really liked both its design and comfort. I collected them all over a period of time and, even when I gave away two pairs, I made sure they were replaced, and that was when it finally hit me that I had a problem with shoe collection! (God has all sorts of children, and I am one that's being cleansed and purified).

As I stood by the doorway to my bedroom, my eyes fell on all these boxes of shoes, and it dawned on me that I even had

The Ten Wise and Foolish Virgins (Which group do you belong)?

some in the collection that were up to ten years old, still new and had never been worn! I looked at all of them for a while and also looked at the visible ones around other areas of the room, and I said to myself, "You know what? The real chief priest of worldliness is sitting right here in your bedroom! What in the world are you doing with all these shoes that you hardly wear, anyway?" There I was - a Christian, having the effrontery to judge part of the body of Christ of worldliness when the chief priest of it had been resident within me all this time. Exactly what did I expect to see in a growing church with new and dear Christian brothers and sisters trooping out of the world into the church? The spirit of holiness? They were coming as they were, saved by grace and mercy just as I have been, tromping into the house of the Lord, where they will eventually be cleansed of worldliness by the water of the word just as I am still being cleansed. Instead of rejoicing with heaven for these precious souls that were coming back home to the Father, I had the effrontery to judge them when I was no better, or different, myself! I had allowed religion to rub off on me without even realising it. So I repented genuinely before God that day for my judgemental attitude towards his church and my dear brothers and sisters. I have no doubt at all that some, or most, of them have even grown up better than I have spiritually because they have a good and stable teacher of the word of God leading them. I also repented of my unusual addiction to shoe collection. Sometimes we carry things like this in us without realising it, and it takes the word of God and the Spirit of the Lord to help us see that we may turn away from it! Not that loving shoes and buying them is wrong, but whenever fleshly habits seem to override your will and wisdom and you are not checking or controlling them, that means you are lacking good self and spiritual discipline.

The Lord says, in John 14:6, "I am the way - [the cross and the blood], the truth - [the word], and the Life - [the Spirit]. No one comes to the father except through me." The Bible makes it very clear that:

1. We cannot mock God, as every man will reap what he sows (Galatians 6:7).
2. We are to take up our crosses daily and follow Christ!

The reason for this is because the Cross represents crucifixion, and the reason we are to take them up daily is because, as we go about our daily lives, we should be prepared and willing to lay the cross down, lie on it, and be crucified to whatever it is that is not of God in us, as we come across these things in our lives and the Holy Spirit convicts us of it in our daily walk!

Matthew 10:38 says, "He who does not take his cross and follow after me is not worthy of me."

We have to be willing to lay it all down just as Christ laid it all down for us. As Jesus says in Mark 8:34, "...whoever desires to come after me, let him deny himself and take up his cross and follow me."

The problem with so many of us, however, is that we are unwilling to deny ourselves. The flesh does not take kindly to denial or discipline, but our will is the determining factor. To whom do you yield it? Self or the word and the Spirit of the Lord within you? Our will is our strength; hence, the Bible says to love the Lord with all of our strength (Mk 12:30), which is the first commandment. When we love the Lord with our strength, we will have no problem submitting our will to Him and letting His Holy Spirit in us take control. We do, or manifest, whatever we **yield** our will to do. Once we yield our will to do something, we automatically give our strength to manifest it.

Sadly enough, some of the preaching that comes out of the pulpit these days has become so liberal, as some of our gospel ministers would rather not rock, let alone shake, the boat so as not to offend people or make them too uncomfortable so that they want to leave the church. The more people that come and stay in the church, the more increase in church funds for those that give, and it presents a good image to have large congregations - the larger the better. These pastors would rather follow the psychological concept of dealing with people because "times are changing," and the Church should learn to change with the times, even if the occurrences of the times are becoming more and more God-desensitized and against God's moral codes or standard.

The God we serve, however, is a God that changes not! He is the same yesterday today and forever (Hebrews 13:8). Neither has He changed His mind about any of His written word! The Bible declares that Heaven and Earth will pass away, but His word will not pass away (Matt 24:35)! It is also written that, "My words have I magnified above my name" (Ps 138:2). That is how very seriously God takes his word! Despite all of the great and many names of God, He magnifies His word more than His name, and if God Himself magnifies His word more than His own name, then how are we as Christians treating the word of God? That is a question for all of us to answer in our hearts. Consider, for a moment, the words of Christ in Matthew 5:17-20. "Do not think that I came to destroy the law and the prophets. I did not come to destroy, but to fulfil [i.e., to live it out]." Thereby, Jesus showed us how to walk the word also.

Some of us also like to stay and play it safe within our church walls. We bury our heads in the sand and do not declare sin as sin because we are afraid of persecution. Whether we are prepared for it or not, persecution will come. The earlier we start to fall on our faces before God and pray, cry out for the "Spirit of prayer" to fall on us like never before so that there will be such an outcry of prayer from God's people to the throne room of heaven such as has never been heard before since the creation of mankind to date, the earlier we will receive the strength and help of God for our time of need. We need to shake the heavens and the earth with the power of prayer so that there will be realignment in the heavens and on the earth, even as the events of the book of Revelation begin to unfold.

The Bible declares that the *effectual fervent* prayer of a righteous man *avails much* (James 5:16). This is very true, even if some of us do not fully understand it. Also the Bible declares that, "If my people [not the world, but his people-us as Christians] that are called by my name will humble themselves and pray and seek my face and turn from their wicked ways [compromise and the way of the world], then I will hear from heaven and will forgive their sin and heal their land" (2 Chronicles 7:14)

The onus is on God's people that are called by His name, not on the world!

As far as I know, and with the little the Lord has permitted me to see behind the scenes, no matter how much a man believes he knows God, I am convinced that he has not truly known Him until he sees Him in battle for His own (His covenant people), to honour His word and His name! It is a very fearsome scene!

Chapter 5

Our Paths

The Lord told me recently during an intercessory prayer meeting that a lot of his servants - rather than teaching and preaching to His people about how to walk in the fear of the Lord, live holy before God for He is holy, rather than build upon His altars the fires of holiness and the fear of the Lord, have built for themselves pedestals based on avarice! I was not sure what "avarice," meant as the Holy Spirit often leads me in prophetic intercession, and I often hear the message for the first time as it comes out of my mouth in the spirit, and the interpretation immediately follows.

After the prayer ended, I asked my prayer partner what "avarice" meant, and she did not know either, so we got the dictionary and it interpreted it as 'extreme greed for wealth'. I was shocked. He also said they have led His children into bondages that He has not purposed for them through their unbalanced teachings on the message of prosperity. He went on to explain and reveal a lot to me about what was happening behind the financial scenes. He said, as it was in the day of Naomi, so it will be upon those who have not waited upon His word and for His timing, who have gone on to do business with the world that He has not set for them. I asked him how it was in Naomi's day, as I remembered that she lost everything, and He said she felt that nothing was happening during the famine and she left Bethlehem (the house of bread – the word) to go to Moab a type

Our Paths

of the world – a place where, she believed, things would be better. She did this instead of remaining in Bethlehem, trusting in, and waiting on the Lord and his time of manifestation. She however, came back empty-handed.

The Lord said so many will return empty-handed because they have gone after their lust and greed by going the way of the world. Because many of his servants have thought the message of prosperity out of balance and out of their greed, so many have come to focus on His hands rather than His heart and His will. Instead of them seeking God the giver, they sought the gifts without having the needed character to carry it. When they felt that it was not happening quickly enough, they trooped out and got involved with the world, compromising His word and expecting Him to come out and bless what He had not sent them to do in the first place! When things begin to fall apart, the love of many will begin to wax cold, not only because the evil one will engineer this through abominations, but also because the people will become disillusioned and disappointed - not only from not seeing the reaping of their sowings, but also because their expectations will begin to fall apart before their very eyes, despite the truth of the word of God that says the expectation of a <u>righteous</u> man shall not be cut off. This, however, need not be so if we will return to the cross and the blood. The Lord is merciful and will abundantly pardon. In His judgement, He remembers His mercy when we cry out for it. Those who have been faithful however, need not fear because the Lord of hosts is their covering!

He talked much on mortgages, and I asked Him why He was so particular about it (He sounded grieved and impatient or irritated). He said because so many have put themselves in the bondage that He has not wanted them to be in. I tried to explain the economic sense that I have heard concerning taking out a mortgage, rather than paying rent, and I even reminded him about Christians coming out to give testimonies about how the Lord has blessed them with their own house bought with a mortgage. He swung around and, with what I can only describe as a gentle but irritated voice, asked me, "How can I bless my own people with a curse"? It is a curse to be enslaved when He paid a price for our freedom - the price of His very precious blood. He said, "have you not read that 'the borrower will be servant to the lender?' And 'the rich *rule* over the poor'?" (bold and italics mine because he stressed the word) - (Prov. 22:7). He made me see that they have borrowed indirectly from the enemy's camp unaware. He asked me how I think the enemy will want to see them free; especially those he knows are of Him.

He told me that an economy crash was coming, and when the real one hit, people would go to bed believing everything was ok as they would be adjusting themselves in anxiety of what would be going on, but they would wake up and all their life's investments would be gone. He said many would lose their homes and all they have ever worked for. There would be a great recession and it would be worse than Black Friday and the Great Depression. I did wonder what Black Friday and great depression meant afterwards until a man of God, who is also an accountant by profession, explained them to me. When I researched it further, I discovered that September 24th, 1869 - which was a Friday - was a day the markets crashed following a failed attempt by some financiers to corner the gold market and this led to a crash which brought on a deep recession named Black Friday. The great depression was after world war 11. It started in 1930 and lasted for some years.

He said many would become homeless, as they would lose their home en masse, and there would be much chaos and confusion.

He told me all these in 2005 before the current recession first hit and, when I began to see some of the things I saw in the vision as He was talking, I asked Him if this was the Black Friday type thing he had been talking about, and he said "no"- that "they just tested the waters with this one". He said, after some time, it would look as if things have started to pick up again (as the people will be lied to and deceived), and people will start to heave a sigh of relief and start to relax again. Then, just when they are starting to adjust themselves, they will be hit out of the blue with various others so bad that it will rock the very foundations of people's confidence and faith.

He said the recession was being orchestrated from behind the scenes in other to prepare the people and put them in the position that the enemy wants them in, before he manifests himself on the scene as the leader of the one world government. He could not achieve that in Heaven and he was cast out, so he is determined to achieve it on earth by working through a shadow government that controls most of the ones we see, like puppets on a strings. He controls them through terror, fear, lies, deception, blackmail, manipulations, greed, lusts and lack of true knowledge. Now they pass laws that that are contrary to God's laws and plot against the Lord and his people according to the plan of the enemy because he knows his time is short. They claim to have superior hidden knowledge to rule and manipulate the world for their master's purpose, a world they did not create. A world that God created for himself and for his purpose, but here are the words of the Lord –

1 Corinthians 1:27
But God has chosen the foolish things of the world **to put to shame the wise**, and God has chosen the weak things of the world to put to **shame the things which are mighty;**

The Bible declares in Psalms 2

Why do the nations rage,
And the people plot a vain thing?
2 The kings of the earth set themselves,
And the rulers take counsel together,
Against the Lord and against His Anointed, saying,
3 "Let us break Their bonds in pieces
And cast away Their cords from us."

**4 He who sits in the heavens shall laugh;
The Lord shall hold them in derision.
5 Then He shall speak to them in His wrath,
And distress them in His deep displeasure:**
6 "Yet I have set My King
On My holy hill of Zion."

7 "I will declare the decree:
The Lord has said to Me,
'You are My Son,
Today I have begotten You.
8 Ask of Me, and I will give You
The nations for Your inheritance,
And the ends of the earth for Your possession.
9 You shall break[a] them with a rod of iron;
You shall dash them to pieces like a potter's vessel.'"

10 Now therefore, be wise, O kings;
Be instructed, you judges of the earth.
11 Serve the Lord with fear,
And rejoice with trembling.
12 Kiss the Son,[b] lest [c] He be angry,
And you perish in the way,
When His wrath is kindled but a little.
Blessed are all those who put their trust in Him.
(Bold mine)

    I asked Him what would happen to the Christians and began to plead with Him to do something. He said that, if they had paid attention to His word by seeking out the truth for themselves like the Berean Christians and prayed for revelation and understanding, if they had waited for His timing in obedience, if they had not lived more in the flesh and after the flesh, if they had sought His face and His will rather than his hand, if they had not allowed themselves to be blown about with every wind of doctrines some of which had come from leaders with great greed for wealth and also from leaders who are wolves in sheep's clothing, then they would not have been in the way of what is going to hit.
    I said, "Yes, Lord, but you can do something. He paused and looked ahead intently then said, "except they return to the cross and the blood, there are dark and hard days ahead." I felt He stressed the words **dark** and **hard**. I meditated on these things afterwards and began to understand, by the help of the Holy Spirit, that the cross is a place of repentance. It is the place

where we turn away from sin and lay it all down at the foot of the cross. Even if you have done it before and walked away from keeping it up, do it again!

Returning to the blood is honouring the blood in our lives with the utmost reverence. It is the shed blood of our Lord which redeemed us from death. It is the blood of God's covenant with His people. It is a covering over us as children of God, abiding in His word and letting His word abide in us.

It is a hedge of divine protection over our lives, and there is absolutely nothing that the enemy can do about it. We are the only ones who can create the doorway in this hedge by a life of continuous disobedience – a life of sin. It was the blood that protected the land of Goshen where the Israelites lived in Egypt. They stayed within the confines of it after they applied it. The blood of Jesus is the same yesterday, today and tomorrow. The Lord is always merciful when we genuinely repent and cry out for his mercy.

The Bible says, in Prov. 10:8, "…whoever breaks the hedge, the serpent will bite!" Some of us just keep breaking the hedge of divine protection around us through sin. We repent and do it again, and this goes on in a seemingly endless circle. What we do not realise, however, is that when we repent and plead the blood covering, the blood hedge is covered again and again, and we are cleansed from all unrighteousness, according to the Bible because God is faithful. However, what about the poison of the serpent after we have been bitten? The poison is not the unrighteousness. It is the after-effect of breaking the hedge. The poison and its effect, is the result of breaking the hedge; hence, it is written that we cannot mock God, as every man will reap what he sows (Gal. 6:7)!

Earlier in the book of Galatians (5:1), the Bible tells us to, "Stand fast, therefore, in the liberty by which Christ has made us free, and do not be entangled again with a yoke of bondage! Later in that same chapter, in verse sixteen, we learn, "…walk in the spirit, and you shall not fulfil the lust of the flesh. Paul, in his letter to the Romans, asks the question, "Do you not know that to whom you present yourself slaves to obey? You are that one's slave whom you obey, whether of sin leading to death or of obedience leading to righteousness" (6:16).

We NEED to learn to honour the name of Jesus, His word, and His blood in our lives with the utmost reverence. A threefold cord is not easily broken (Eccl.4:12). We honour it by a life of reverential fear and obedience to His word. We honour it by the way we represent His name here on earth and before the heavens. We honour it by the utmost appreciation, gratitude and an inestimable value of what His blood has done, and is still doing, for us. We cannot continue to violate this with impunity and behave like spoilt brats and expect to walk in victory! Hebrews10:26 declare, "For if we sin wilfully after we have received the knowledge of the truth, there no longer remains a sacrifice for sin."

Anyone who rejects the law of Moses dies without mercy on the testimony of two or three witnesses. Of how much worse punishment do you suppose will be thought worthy one who has trampled the son of God underfoot, counted the blood of the covenant by which he was sanctified a common thing, and insulted the Spirit of grace? For we know him who said "vengeance in mine, I will repay," and again the Lord will judge his people. It is a fearful thing to fall into the hands of the living God!

The book of Romans, chapter 6, is one of the passages of scripture that I believe every Christian who truly desires to grow should constantly read and meditate upon until revelation and understanding comes, and this will give them sound knowledge. Knowledge is power, if you are ready and willing to apply it for good. I believe that the main reason so many of us struggle so hard is because we have not taken enough time to know who we truly are in Christ, and we can only know this from His word and a true and intimate personal relationship with Him! When we come to this understanding, we will operate differently. The more we see and understand who we truly are in Christ, the more we will recoil from the desire or temptation to sin! Sin will become repulsive to us.

When David sinned, he repented. God forgave him, but he still reaped the consequence of his actions. When we sin and ask God to forgive us, He does so out of His faithfulness, and the record is no longer on our page book in heaven, but because we have already sown the seed, we reap its harvest; hence, it is written that God is not mocked. Whatever a man sows, he shall also reap (Gal 6:7)! When we break the hedge through sin and get bitten by the serpent, we repent. The hedge is sealed again, but we are left carrying the poison of the serpent, so to speak. The blood of Christ cleanses us from all unrighteousness, as it is written, but I don't believe that it also takes away the consequence of *continuous* and wilful deliberate sin. So the habitual cycle of knowingly and wilfully committing sin and repenting when we know that we have the power through Christ to overcome won't do us any good. Besides, when the word of God tells us to stay away from sin, it for our own utmost good and protection. This might seem like it is conflicting the message of grace.

It is not. Grace empowers us or enables us, but it does not change God's law that declares in Genesis 8:22 "While the earth remains, **Seedtime and harvest,** Cold and heat, Winter and summer, And day and night **Shall not cease."** (bold and italics, mine)

The Bible makes it clear that sin no longer has dominion over us because we are not under, law, but under grace! So we have the power through the blood, the Word and the Spirit to overcome sinful habits.

Romans 6:12-14 puts it this way, "Therefore do not let sin reign in your mortal body, that you should obey it in its lusts. And do not present your members as instruments of unrighteousness to sin, but present yourselves to God as being alive from the dead, and your members as instruments of righteousness to God. **For sin shall not have dominion over you, for you are not under law but under grace."**

Whether we obey God or not do not change God from being God, nor does it affect any of His attributes. He is already who He is and will continue to be for all eternity! It is for our own good because, when we deliberately sin or disobey God's word and do not repent, we create unnecessary doorways of entrance for the enemy into our lives. Even Job with his record had **fear** as a doorway. The Bible says the fearful shall have their part in the lake which burns with fire and brimstone (Rev.21:8). I did wonder why the fearful were named among these until it dawned on me that, if we are fearful, that means we doubt God's word and promises to us. Simply put, we do not trust God, and this infers that His words and promises cannot be true, which makes him out to be a liar.

Every word written concerning us in the Bible it true. We are who and what the Bible declares that we are. It is a spiritual foregone conclusion. To begin to experience and manifest it however, we have to know it by studying it, believing it, and agree with it. We must meditate on it regularly confess it and **choose** to **yield** ourselves to it irrespective of whether it makes sense to us or not, and whether we feel like it or not. Just trust and obey, period!

Even the Angels are amazed and rejoice when we manifest some mysteries by the power of the Holy Spirit because of the blood covenant. God's angels have no blood covenant with Him. The only time I have had the opportunity to study the features of an Angel at very close proximity, though the Lord permits me to see them now and again, was during a time the Holy Spirit was teaching me a tactic in spiritual warfare prayer. As I did what He asked and enabled me to do, the Angel that was standing on the left side of the Lord Jesus on a platform bent over and looked at me with an expression of curiosity on his face. I had never seen that look on an angel's face before and I am yet to see it again. I have seen them looking stern in time of crises and warfare. I have even seen them smiling and dancing, but never with an expression of curiosity. He bent over to see what I was doing by the power of the Holy Spirit and the effect it was creating, his face came very close to mine and I had the first and only opportunity so far to study an Angel's face and wings at close quarters. Except all Angels are identical which I doubt, I believe I will recognise this particular one in Heaven, or when next I see him. When I asked the Holy Spirit why he was looking at me like that, as I was puzzled myself, He gave me Peter 1:12 and Ephesians 3:9-11.

"Of this salvation the prophets have inquired and searched carefully, who prophesied of the grace that would come to you, searching what, or what manner of time, the Spirit of Christ who was in them was indicating when He testified beforehand the sufferings of Christ and the glories that would follow. To them it was revealed that, not to them, but to us they were ministering the things which now have been reported to you through those who have preached the gospel to you by the Holy Spirit sent from heaven—*things which angels desire to look into*" (bold and italics mine)
(1 peter 1:10-12).

Eph 3:8-12 says, "...And to make all see what is the fellowship of the mystery, which from the beginning of the ages has been hidden in God who created all things through Jesus Christ. To the intent that now the manifold wisdom of God be made known to the Church, the principalities and powers in heavenly places according to the eternal purpose which he accomplished **in Christ Jesus our Lord."**

When the whole experience was over, I looked the passages up in the Bible and understood.

Chapter 6

The Cross and the Blood

*T*he Lord told me recently that some ministers even now hesitate to preach and teach about the Blood, as they consider it old-fashioned, and they want to move along with the worldly trend. They hesitate to declare sin as sin and do not teach holiness and the fear of the Lord. I could not believe my ears - not because I thought the Lord would lie, as it is impossible for him to do so, but because I began to wonder what their calling was based on, if they felt or thought that they could do away with the Blood. I was quite shocked and He made it very clear that except they return to the way of the Cross and the Blood, most won't go far, nor will they be able to withstand the days ahead because there are hard days ahead! He made a statement that has stuck with me till this day. He said "the Cross and the Blood is our BANNER OF SALVATION AND OUR EMBLEM OF VICTORY." Now I know what Banner and Emblem are, but I still meditate upon that statement often, as I know that I have not yet grasped its full meaning. I am still asking the Lord to minister more to me on that point.

As for returning to the cross and the blood, it for us to constantly remember from where we came, the great price that was paid for our redemption, and the victory that has been handed down to us. When we constantly remember this as our foundation, it then becomes a must and a determination for, and in, us to constantly honour this great sacrifice and reverently walk in the victory of the blood through a constant life of reverential obedience to His word and His will.

It is written, "and they overcame him by the blood of the lamb and the word of their testimony." Not by the position they held in church, or how often they were in church or prayer meetings or seminars. Not even by how much they preached the word of God or how popular they were in ministry, but by the BLOOD OF THE LAMB and the WORD OF THEIR TESTIMONY! How much are you honouring the shed blood of Christ for you in your life, and to what are you testifying? His word, the situation you see, or what controlled society is dictating to you in the name of political correctness?

What brings us into the kingdom of God is the Spirit of the living God that draws us, the word of faith we hear, and the blood sacrifice that we accept and surrender to. What keeps us in the kingdom of God is the Spirit of the living God, the word of God we abide in, and the blood of Christ that continues to cleanse us. Hence, when we remain in the Spirit and continuously declare his word as it is written, irrespective of what we see, we then overcome by the blood of the lamb and by the word of our testimony!

The Lord also said there are many of His servants that claim him to be their source, but deep in their hearts, their source is their congregation and what they generate from them. He said that, when trying times come, their true source will be revealed. He said it is the congregation member that has enough to eat that will remember his Minister. He said His true servants at this end time will be the chosen ones that have truly died to the lust of the flesh, eyes and the pride of life.

They will be those that will rise early to seek the face of the Heavenly Father in their private places, and they will come away from His presence with a Glory covering, and whatever they need, will be made manifest to them as at when they need it. He said that was how He did it waking up early to be before the father and after He was done, whatever He needed was made manifest right when he needed it. He said it is written that many are called, but few are chosen. He said that it is those that choose to go all the way, irrespective of the persecutions or

The Ten Wise and Foolish Virgins (Which group do you belong)?

how narrow the path is, - those that are willing to lay it all down for the kingdom's sake and the will of the Father, - those that choose all of God, they are the ones that the Lord will choose right back! He said, but these are not many as not many are willing to fully die to themselves. I then understood the scripture as I had always wondered why the Lord will call many, but only choose a few. He reminded me that what you sow, you reap!

When we choose to continue to walk in the way of our flesh and self, rather than in the way of the word of God and the leading of His Spirit, we trample underfoot the very precious price the Lord paid for our redemption. When a man becomes born again, old things pass away, and all things become new spiritually; hence, we are required to walk in this newness of life, and the only way we can succeed at that is by renewing our minds with the word of God and CHOOSING to walk and live in it.

Not too long ago, two people very close to me were in very bad situations. Before it started, I dreamt of it and knew there was a very rough time ahead, and I warned them. The situation, however, affected me deeply because of my involvement with them, and I began to fast and pray. One day, my praying got so deeply intense and I was in agony of soul for these two people, that I began to groan in the spirit, as no words were coming out anymore.

I do not know how long I had been doing that, but slowly I began to experience a very strange tingling sensation all over my skin. It felt as if my pores were being stretched out, and it was getting quite uncomfortable, so I started to rub down my skin with the open palms of my hands in an attempt to calm it down, but the sensation only grew more intense and very uncomfortable. I became concerned, as I had never experienced anything like it before. When it was almost unbearable, I asked the Holy Spirit what was going on, and He told me it was the same experience that Christ went through in the garden of Gethsemane before he started to sweat blood. That shocked me more than any spiritual experience I have ever had, and a great reverential fear and grief came upon me.

First, I feared that I would start bleeding like Christ, as I know that the Lord did not need my blood to answer my prayer. The only blood needed had already been shed by Christ. Two, I felt grief that Jesus had gone through a similar and more intense agony of soul for us in the flesh until he started to bleed and eventually laid his life down for us. I became totally broken and began to weep, no longer for the people I was praying for, but for the realisation that He went through a more intense experience, even unto death for me, you - if you are born again and even for those who do not yet know Him. To date, that experience continues to give me a seriously reverential fear and humbleness of heart, and it draws me even more closely to the Lord.

I believe with all of my heart, that if every Spirit-filled Christian that is finding it difficult to die to self and yield to God goes through this kind of experience; we won't need too much teaching on the fear of God and obedience to the word. We will get there much quicker! Why the Lord allowed me to experience that, I do not know. Maybe I needed it, as it has now caused me to be highly reverential of the sacrifice that He went through for me, and it just causes my heart to seek after Him like never before. I am not quite sure how to put it into words because even writing about it now makes my heart feel very raw. All I can say further is that the sacrifice He made for our redemption is far too great for us not to honour it in total surrender and obedience to Him.

We NEED the teaching of the shed BLOOD OF CHRIST FOR US AND HOW TO HONOUR IT IN OUR LIVES IN TOTAL SURRENDER TO HIS WILL AND OBEDIENCE TO HIS WORD, MUCH MORE THAN TEACHING ON PROSPERITY! That is, we need to be reminded to seek first His kingdom and His righteousness, and the prosperity will be added because it is already ours by right of the shed blood of Christ! As it is written, "seek <u>FIRST</u> **the kingdom of God** and <u>HIS RIGHTEOUSNESS</u> and all these things shall be added unto you!" (Matt 6:33).

More recently, there have been teachings in some quarters to seek the prosperity first before we consider his righteousness; that is, if we are willing to die, and so many of us are not! No wonder we are not seeing much prosperity, but instead, we are seeing stagnation and frustration. We won't see much in the way of prosperity until we go back and do it in the correct order of the word of God!

I told the Lord, after He told me to write and finish this book that I don't think this message will be popular, and He replied that He had not called me to a popularity contest, and that I should write what He has been revealing to me, and those who desire truth and choose to listen will hear.

The Bible tells us in Matthew 6:31-33, 'Therefore do not worry, saying what shall we eat? Or what shall we drink." We are to seek FIRST **THE KINGDOM OF GOD** and **His RIGHTEOUSNESS** and all the things that we need shall be added unto us.(Bold, mine)

The problem some of us have is that we come into the kingdom and, instead of following in the next step of seeking **HIS RIGHTEOUSNESS**; we begin to seek by ourselves all the other stuff that is to be added for free! We are not meant to seek the other stuff. We are meant to seek after His righteousness instead, and what we desire will be added for FREE, according to His will! If we will understand this and allow it to become rooted in us, we will come into His rest and will focus our attention on seeking His righteousness through His word and will have a continuously deeper walk with him, by the help of the Holy Spirit.

We are already the righteousness of God in Christ Jesus, according to 2 Corinthians 5:21, "For He made Him who knew no sin to be sin for us, that we might become the righteousness of God in Him." However, we are called to live out our righteousness! Hence, there is no more excuse for sin. We could never establish our own righteousness by works. Instead, we must accept Christ's, by faith, and walk in it! Two of Paul's epistles speak to this truth.

Romans 10:3
"For they, being ignorant of God's righteousness, and seeking to establish their own righteousness, have not submitted to the righteousness of God."

<u>1 Corinthians 15:34</u>
"**<u>Awake</u>** to righteousness, and **<u>do not sin</u>**; for some do not have the knowledge of God. I speak this to your shame. (Underline and bold mine)."

The Bible says in John 15:7, "If you abide in me and my words abide in you, you will ask what you desire and it shall be done for you!" So simple, but oftentimes, the subtle pride in us and misplaced faith often hinders us from accepting the simplicity of the gospel, and we end up again in works instead of staying in simple childlike faith in a most gracious Heavenly Father!

To abide means to continue in, to wait on, trust in, persevere in, to stay in, Simply put, live in the **WORD, and allow** it to **live in you**, that **you may be able** to live by it!

Are you asking the Lord for your heart's desire, and are not getting any response? Maybe you should check the depths of your abiding in His word and how much you let His word abide in you.

If you are sure that you are not lacking in that area, then **TRUST Him**! He knows what is best for you, and He knows the perfect timing!

The Bible also says, in Proverbs16:7, that when a man's ways please the Lord, He will make even his enemies to be at peace with him! I believe it is wisdom to concentrate on making our ways pleasing to God. That way we will not have to disturb ourselves about which enemy is after us, nor strive so much against them! I know a good deal when I see one, and I believe this is one of the best!

The Crucifixion and the Blood have redeemed us into a newness of, and a new way of life. It is our responsibility to yield our will [strength] to the Holy Spirit and let him lead us in this newness and new way of life (Romans 6:1-16). That is why the "new wine had to be poured into a new wine skin." The spirit of the Lord has to come into our newly recreated spirit (Luke 5:28).

The Bible tells us to work out our salvation with fear and trembling (Phil 2:12)! **The responsibility is ours** to do so. The

The Ten Wise and Foolish Virgins (Which group do you belong)?

word is there to guide us and the Holy Spirit will always be there to help us through if we are willing. His grace will empower us.

As I have previously explained, the Bible tells us that, "Don't you know that to whom you yield your will to obey, you are that one's slave whom you obey, whether of sin leading to death or of obedience leading to righteousness" (Romans 6:16). Your will is your strength, and whatever or whomever you yield it to, dictates what will manifest. God, Jesus and the Holy Spirit will not override our will. Neither can the devil! **We CHOOSE** whom or what, we yield it to, and true wisdom says that we yield it to God. In that, we stay safe and are protected.

This does not mean that we will not stumble now and again. The Lord knows about all the stumbling we would do before we were born. When we stumble, we should be quick to repent and move on. It is when we camp at our place of stumbling that it becomes a problem. The Lord does not look at us through our stumbling, but through the blood of Christ. He sees us in Him and we are made perfect in Him

In the gospel of John, the first miracle the Lord performed was turning water into wine. In that parable was part of the picture of his ministry.

> "On the third day there was a wedding in Canaan of Galilee and the mother of Jesus was there. Now both Jesus and His disciples [The bridegroom and the bride – his disciples – the Church] were invited to the wedding. And when they ran out of wine, the mother of Jesus said to Him, "They have no wine [representing the Holy Spirit]." Jesus said to her, "Woman, what does your concern have to do with Me? My hour [of manifestation] has not yet come." His mother said to the servants, "Whatever He says to you, do it [obey every word of God]." Now there were set there six water pots of stone, according to the manner of purification of the Jews, containing twenty or thirty gallons apiece. Jesus said to them "Fill the water pots with water." And they filled them up to the brim. And He said to them, "Draw some out now, and take it to the master of the feast." And they took it. When the

The Cross And The Blood

master of the feast had tasted the water that was made wine, and did not know where it came from (but the servants who had drawn the water knew), the master of the feast called the bridegroom. And he said to him, "Every man at the beginning sets out the good wine, and when the guests have well drunk, then the inferior. You have kept the good wine until now!"
(John 2:1-10, NKJV).

To start with, from what I learnt according to Jewish culture, "My hour has not yet come" meant hour of presentation. That is, it was not yet time for Jesus to present whatever drink He and His family had brought to the wedding. Secondly, the tradition of purification was according to man-made tradition and not according to the Torah. It was not part of God's law. So the Lord was breaking the added tradition to God's law. According to tradition, it was abominable for wine to even touch the water pots, let alone sit inside to be drawn. That is the logos of the passage. The Rhema, however, is much deeper.

A careful study of this first miracle in the book of John will reveal a parallel of our salvation walk which will end with us, the Church, as Bride. In other words, think of it as the five wise virgins meeting with Christ, the Bridegroom.

There was a joining together of a Bride with her Groom at this wedding. They had run out of wine. The Jewish people had gone their own way, doing their religious rituals away from the Torah (Word) of the Lord that was originally given to them.

Jesus' mother told His disciples, "Whatever He says to you, do it..." That meant that they were to show full Obedience to His words and commandments.

There were six water pots – six representing the number of man, and water representing the word of God. They were obviously empty (lacking the true knowledge and revelation of the word of God).

He asked them to "FILL" the water pots with water.

They were only used for purification (man-made religious) rituals. When we lack, or reject, the true knowledge of the word of God, we end up with religion instead of relationship with the Lord.

Water, according to Ephesians 5:26, represents the WORD OF GOD. Jesus' disciples filled the pots to the brim and, when they were drawn out at the Lord's command, the water had turned into wine!

The disciples in the book of Acts were preaching and teaching the word. People were receiving and getting filled with the word, and there were manifestations of the Holy Spirit with signs following. The infilling and indwelling of the WORD of God in us produces the manifestations of the HOLY SPIRIT, which the wine represents. See Isaiah 55:1 and Proverbs 9:2 below. These are prophetic scriptures about the word of God and His Spirit. The word and the Holy Spirit are freely given.

Isaiah 55:1 declares in prophecy, "Ho! Everyone who thirsts, come to the waters [the word]; And you who have no money come buy and eat." In other words, it's free. Yes, come buy wine [The Spirit] and milk [1 Pet.2:2, - the word] without money and without price because they have been freely given to you by the Lord.

Prov.9:1-6 says, "Wisdom has slaughtered her meat [the word], she has mixed her wine [the Holy Spirit], she has also furnished her table [blessings]. She has sent out her maidens [disciples], she cries out from the highest places of the city [proclaiming the good news]. Whoever is *simple*, let him turn in here [Psalm 119:130 - the entrance of Your words gives light;

It gives understanding to the *simple*.]. As for him who lacks understanding, she says to him, come eat of my bread [the word], and drink of the wine I have mixed [the Holy Spirit]. Forsake foolishness and live! And go in the way of understanding!" (Italics mine).

Chapter 7

The Spirit and the Word

The Spirit of the Lord and His word go together. First John 5:7-8 declares, "there are three that bears witness in Heaven - The Father, the WORD, and the Holy Spirit, and these three are ONE ; there are three that bears witness on Earth, the Spirit, the Word and the Blood, these three agree as one."

Proverbs 9:1-6 declares, "Wisdom has built her house [the Church], she has hewn out her seven pillars [the seven church ages]. "Wisdom has slaughtered her MEAT [the word - [12] For when for the time ye ought to be teachers, ye have need that one teach you again which be the first principles of the oracles of God; and are become such as have need of milk, and not of **strong meat.**

[13] For every one that useth milk is unskilful in the word of righteousness: for he is a babe.
[14] But **strong meat** belongeth to them that are of full age, even those who by reason of use have their senses exercised to discern both good and evil. (Hebrews 5:12-14- King James version).

She, Wisdom, had mixed her wine [the Holy Spirit]."

The Word cannot manifest without the Holy Spirit, and the Holy Spirit will rarely manifest without, or outside of the word. They always go together, and it is the Word that we have on the inside of us that the Holy Spirit will quicken to us when we need it. Hence it is **most important** that we have the **word of God** stored in us more than anything else in our lives. Also, it is not just enough to have the word stored in us until it becomes an issue of pride and we feel that we know it all and use the Word as a whip on others instead of as a tool of Love used in Humility and Grace.

I have come across some brothers and sisters like that. They are so knowledgeable in the word and wield it like a whip, and no one wants to listen to them because they may have the word, but there is no fruit of it in their lives. They do not minister it in love; hence, the Bible says to receive the Word with MEEKNESS! We should be humble enough to let the Word have its way with us first, so that it will bear fruit IN LOVE! I can't stress this enough. I have hardly come across anyone who rejects genuine Love. They might initially be suspicious of your motives, depending on their mind set, but as soon as they realise it's for real, they always come around in the end. The Bible says "Love conquers ALL" (1 Corinthians 13).

It is our total agreement and submission to the Word of God and the Holy Spirit that will bring us to that point. The Bible says, "How can two walk together except they agree?" (Amos 3:3).

The Lord also said, "Love the Lord your God with all your heart [the seat of your emotions], mind [your intellect], soul [self], and strength [will}]" (Mark 12:30-21 and Luke 10:27). And the Bible also tells us to "love your neighbour as yourself." In other words, DO UNTO OTHERS AS YOU WOULD WANT THEM TO DO UNTO YOU!!!!

The Lord told me once to treat others exactly as I would want them to treat me, and I have done everything within my understanding, by His grace, to live like that.

Most of us have at the back of our minds that the salvation walk is a difficult one (especially when it begins to conflict with our old nature, or when we come into trials and temptations) despite the truth of God's word that says "my yoke is easy, and my burden is light" (Matt 11:30). What we fail to realize is that our old nature is bound to rebel against any new way that will subject the body or flesh to discipline. This is because habits of our carnal nature have become ingrained in self, and self which is a major part of our soul has always ruled our lives until our spirit man is reborn, and the Lord empowers it by his Spirit to now lead us in a new way of life; that is if we agree to walk in it. The Lord created man in his image and put His Spirit into him to be like God (Gen. 1:26-28), For God said "Let us make man in our image, according to Our likeness; let them have dominion over the fish of the sea, over the birds of the air, and over the cattle, over all the earth and over every creeping thing that creeps on the earth."

Even with that, I believe that he – Adam lacked understanding of his true identity and did not really know who he was because, if he did, he would have known that he was already like God and did not need to yield to the enemy's lies through Eve (Gen 1-6) in order to become what he already was! In his sin, he gave birth to SELF – THE CARNAL NATURE, which is basically selfish and at enmity with God. Sin broke the glory covering over his life; in other words, it separated him from God spiritually.

Notice that, after Adam disobeyed God's commandment by eating the fruit that God forbade him to eat; he suddenly became conscious of self. Prior to this, Adam and Eve were naked and were not ashamed, the Bible says. When people are ashamed, they instinctively cover their faces, or you see the effects of shame on their faces, but both of them covered their loins instead, and when God called out to Adam and asked where he was, his response was, "*I was afraid because I was NAKED and I hid myself*". You would expect that his fear would be because he had done what God commanded him not to do, but instead it was because he was NAKED! (It is the same "*I*" used in this verse that brought Lucifer down, according to the book of Isaiah). Adam now felt exposed and vulnerable.

The devil's plan was to strip the glory covering off them, and since he knows that he cannot touch the glory of God, he had to make Adam and Eve do it by themselves by causing them to doubt the word of God and luring them into disobeying the commandment - to sin. This is exactly the devil's strategy on today's Christians. He has been around a long time and understands the nature of the CARNAL man, but thank God that he is not entitled to the spiritual revelations of God that are given to God's children by his Holy Spirit!

John 3:8
The wind blows where it wishes, and you hear the sound of it, but cannot tell where it comes from and where it goes. *So is everyone who is born of the Spirit."* (Bold and italics, mine)

Satan did exactly the same with the Israelites. when the man of God (Balaam), because of greed for material gains, revealed how to cause the Israelites to stumble, knowing he could not touch the Lord's covering over them, except to get them to do it by themselves (Numbers 31:16 and Rev 2:14). As a spiritual man (a born again, spirit-filled, Bible-believing and abiding Christian) however, he can do very little with you except on the grounds that you permit him to have in your life by your own LACK OF KNOWLEDGE of the truth of the word of God and your CHOICE to walk in disobedience to the truth of the word of God that you know.

"Be angry, and do not sin": do not let the sun go down on your wrath, [27] *nor give place to the devil.*
Ephesians 4:26-27. (Bold and Italics mine).

The Bible says, in Genesis 8:22, "While the earth remains, *Seedtime and harvest,* Cold and heat, Winter and summer, And day and night *shall not cease.*" Even our actions are seeds that we sow, good or bad. Some people may disagree with this point of view, but I advise they study the word and ways of God carefully. I believe that if some non-God fearing and self-loving Christian would actually understand this, they would hesitate to allow themselves to fall into deliberate sin and would be more careful about how they treat others.

When the Lord queried Adam about eating from the fruit, Adam put the blame on Eve, still protecting himself, and Eve put the blame on the serpent, also protecting herself! After all, it was not recorded that the serpent forced her, nor she, Adam. Both of them chose to yield their wills to disobey God's commandment.

Thank God today that our identity is now in Christ who is our role model. Despite this however, so many of us still have an identity crisis. As long as we do not renew our minds with the word of God to reveal who we truly are to us as Christians, for as long as we are not rooted in the knowledge and understanding of who we truly are in Christ, we will be tossed up and down by the enemy. Adam and Eve obviously did not understand, so were easily deceived.

According to Bible scholars, Eve also misrepresented the word three times. She omitted the word "freely", added the words "neither shall you touch it," and she changed "you shall surely die" into "lest you die". The enemy questioned the word of God with Eve, and she misrepresented it. The same enemy questioned the word of God with Christ, and he faithfully repeated it, saying, "IT IS WRITTEN". There is absolutely nothing that the enemy can do with the word of God if we have it on the inside of us, hold onto it faithfully, and confess it boldly. We overcome by the blood of the Lamb and by the word of our testimony; i.e., our confessions, according to, and in agreement with, God's word.

The Lord told Joshua, "Do not let this book of the law depart from your mouth"; i.e., confess in agreement with it all the time! The Israelites also obviously did not know who they truly were as descendants of Abraham, Isaac and Jacob whom God made covenants with, so they were easily taken captive (see Gen 22:15-18) Then the Angel of the LORD called to Abraham a second time out of heaven, [16] and said: "By Myself I have sworn, says the LORD, because you have done this thing, and have not withheld your son, your only *son*— [17] blessing I will bless you, and multiplying I will multiply your descendants as the stars of the heaven and as the sand which *is* on the seashore; **and your descendants shall possess the gate of their enemies**. [18] In your seed all the nations of the earth shall be blessed, because you have obeyed My voice."(bold and italics, mine)

The Ten Wise and Foolish Virgins (Which group do you belong)?

This has also led me to believe that the reason power will be given to the antichrist to overcome the Saints, as mentioned in Daniel 7:25 and Revelation 13:7 will not be because God gives it to him. If he was going to give him power to overcome the Saints at the end, why bother die to give us victory? Why declare that we have been given power to tread upon **ALL** the power of the enemy? "Behold, I give you the authority to trample on serpents and scorpions, and **over all the power of the enemy**, and nothing shall by any means hurt you"(Luke 10:19).

The Lord will not contradict himself. Neither is He an author of confusion. I believe that, it is the Saints that give the Antichrist this power over themselves because of ignorance of who they truly are and their inability to manifest who, and what, they are in Christ Jesus! You cannot manifest what you are not aware of or conscious that you have, or are. The Lord reveals the end from the beginning, and I believe He has revealed this in Genesis in the fall of man and the captivity of Israel in Egypt. Yes, we are expecting revival and great things to happen before Christ comes, but how much EXTRA OIL have we taken in our vessels to keep us burning through the revival and persecution until the catching away or our gathering together to Him?

It was HALF that made it out with the Lord, according to this parable told by the Lord himself - 5 out of 10. Is that not sad, considering the fact that Christ laid his life down for us all as Christians to reconcile us back to the Father?

SO I ASK YOU, WHICH GROUP OF THESE 5 SHOULD YOU BELONG TO? THE CHOICE AND DECISION IS YOURS AND MINE!!!

In Exodus1:8 -14, the Bible says that there arose a new king over Egypt who did not know Joseph. And he said to his people, "Look the children of the people of Israel **are more and mightier than us; come let us deal shrewdly with them, lest they multiply and it happens in the event of war that they also join our enemies and fight against us.**"

The Israelites did not know that they were **more and mightier**, but the enemy knew their strength and chose to deal *shrewdly* with them. I believe that this is exactly what has been happening with the Church of God for quite a long while now. We have the word of God, the authority of the name of Jesus and the power of the blood! Yet so many of us just live and operate within the walls of our own limited spiritual environments, not really knowing our left from our right in the sense that we go to church on Sundays, some during weekdays, as well, and others go the extra mile to conferences. Not very many, however, go all the way or choose to go the extra mile of truly knowing who they are by abiding in the word and letting it renew their minds, dying to the old self and walking in the new identity!

The early church was not as large in number as the church today. They also did not have as much of the written word as we have today. No Christian literature, no huge conferences, no Christian radio nor TV, yet they went on to do great exploits for the kingdom of God with authority that is in the name of Jesus and raw faith. We have all the teachings, I believe, there are on faith, and yet there are not enough manifestations, as would be expected, considering the Christian population today.

I believe, however, that there is coming a great manifestation of the glory and power of God before Christ returns such as has never been seen in the history of Christianity. The Bible declares that the glory of the latter rain will be greater than the former. Much as this is true, let us endeavour now to acquire extra Oil and not wait for the revival before we start to do that.

Remember that the virgins TRIMMED (revived) their lamps–their spirit–yet not all of them had enough Oil to keep their lamps burning for the catching away with Christ to the place of rest in the wilderness away from the persecution. I do not believe that all Christians will go through the end time persecutions. The Lord will protect and preserve those who are truly submitted to him in all things.

I have prayed and meditated on this passage of scripture for so many years, as it has haunted me, so to speak, until the Spirit of the Lord began to speak to me concerning the passage and the Lord finally told me to start writing this book.

The book of Ecclesiastes declares, "There is an evil I have seen under the Sun, as an error proceeding from the ruler; Folly is set in great dignity, while the rich sit in a lowly place I have seen servants on Horses, while princes walk on the ground like servants". This is so true, considering what has been happening with the Church of God for a long while now. The devil was a servant, and so are his descendants, but they have been riding the horses, while most of the Christians, as princes, are walking on the ground like servants out of disobedience and mostly ignorance, except for some that have taken the time to understand their identity and are submitted to God and his word. Things are about to change, however, for those who are on the Lord's side. The Bible says to look on to Jesus, the author and finisher of our faith.

The issue we face becomes twofold, not because the Lord gave us any, but because it now becomes necessary for us to continually renew our minds with God's word and habitually meditate on it so that we gradually begin to manifest the mind of Christ that the Bible declares that we have as born again Christians, instead of our carnal minds. Also, we need to take up our crosses daily and follow Christ by yielding to the gradual crucifixion of our carnal nature! In our habitual meditation upon the word of God, revelation and understanding comes, which produces wisdom for living, if we yield our will to obey it.

The interesting thing however, is that TRUE FREEDOM comes from living according to the word of God - whether it makes sense to us or not, or whether our circumstances are right or wrong.

The Lord says, 'the enemy came and found nothing in me" (John 14:30). That is, there was nothing to lure him with, to attach himself to in Christ, nor was any doorway found in him. The enemy met a dead man walking, so to speak, and that is how we must also learn to walk - by dying daily!

I have come to conclude that true living in freedom in Christ comes only from truly dying to self! So many Christians are either afraid of this, or are hesitant to do so, as we often believe that it is a difficult task to accomplish, so we shift the responsibility to grace, as if grace is what will do it for us. Grace enables us, if we are willing, but it does not override our will. We have to yield our will to obey before grace will take over. If we are not willing, all the grace in the world will accomplish very little for us!

The Lord does not override our will, and neither can the devil. We yield our will to whomever we choose to yield it to. It is within our power - as Christians, in particular, to do so especially when we yield ourselves over to the Holy Spirit (Romans 6:16).

What we see around us may be facts, but the TRUTH of God's word is more than able to overturn those facts. Some of us simply do not understand, or realize, that what we do not have already resident or hidden in us, the devil cannot use to lure or tempt us. The devil cannot succeed at tempting you with what you are already dead, or crucified, to!

The book of James (1:14-15) declares that every man is tempted by **his own lust**; not the devil's own lust, but by the person involved! "But each one is tempted when he is drawn away by *his own* **desires** and enticed. Then, when desire has conceived, it gives birth to sin; and sin, when it is full-grown, brings forth death." [Bold mine]

The Bible says that, when a man's ways are pleasing unto God, He will make even his enemies to be at peace with him (Proverbs 16:7)! Wisdom then teaches me to concentrate on making my ways pleasing unto God by constantly and continuously abiding in Him and in His word, and by obeying Him, so that He will fulfil His part by making my enemy to be at peace with me! That way, I won't have to be constantly trying to fight off the enemy! As I said before, I know a good deal when I see one, and I believe this one is very good.

Chapter 8

The Oil

"Those who were foolish took their lamps and took no oil with them, but the wise took oil in their vessel with their lamps" (Matt 25:3-4).

Since we have already established that lamps represent the spirit of man, what does the Oil represent here? Some people have interpreted it as the anointing, some as grace and some as the Holy Spirit. For a long time, I thought it was the anointing and even taught it so twice and have also heard ministers interpret it as the anointing until the Holy Spirit finally told me that, in this particular passage, it represent the WORD! I was puzzled and began to prayerfully ask for confirmations in the word because the Bible states that in the mouth of two or three witnesses, a matter is established. He took me to Psalms 119:1 to the end and asked me to look at verses 11 and 105 (There's hardly a verse in the whole of Psalm 119 that is not talking of, or about, the word of God!) It is a very good passage for meditation.

Psalm 119:11
"Your word have I hidden in my heart that I might not sin against you."

To keep our lamp burning is a continuous walk of righteousness before God and what enables that is the **word of God** hidden in our hearts – in our spirit. It is the oil that fuels our lamp.

Psalm 119:105
"Your word is a lamp to my feet and a light to my path."

The **word of God** fuels and empowers our lamp-spirit to keep burning that our path and walk in Christ will remain illuminated and we will not stumble. In other words, It shows us which way to walk and in the manner in which we are to walk it.

Now I'd like you to take a look at some important passages dealing with lamps and oil in the Bible—Exodus 27:20 and Proverbs 6:23—and two verses, Colossians 3:16 and Romans 12:2, which tell the Christian how to live in such a way that he will be staying within the will of God.

Exodus 27:20
"And you shall command the children of Israel that they bring you **pure oil** [the purified word of God] **of pressed olive for the light to <u>cause</u> the <u>lamp</u> <u>to burn continually</u> [the spirit of man to remain alight by the word of God and the power of the Holy Spirit].**

This occurs during the care of the lamp stand which you become part of, if you are born again and the Holy Spirit of God lives on the inside of you! We are the temple of the Holy Spirit (1 Cor 3:16)! The Lord says that we are the LIGHT of the world, and you do not light a lamp and put it under a basket, but on a lamp stand, that it may give light to all who are in the house (Matt 5:14-15).

Proverbs 6:23
"For the **commandment is a lamp** and **the law a light**. Reproofs of instruction are the way of life,"

The **word of God** is the oil that fuels the lamp, and a light cannot operate without oil or some sort of fuel, and the **word** is that fuel or oil for every believer. Lamp and fuel have to go together, else the lamp will not work like it is supposed to.

Colossian 3: 16
Let the words of Christ dwell in you richly in all wisdom.

When the word of Christ dwells richly on the inside of us, and we manifest it in wisdom, we show forth ourselves as the true light of the world. The Lord says, "Let your light so shine before men that they may see your good works and glorify your father in heaven."

Romans 12:2.
And do not be conformed to this world, but be *transformed by the renewing of your mind* [with **the word**] that you may proof what is **that good and acceptable and perfect will of God** [through yielding to and obeying the word]. Italics and bracket mine.

This, I believe, is one of the most powerful words in the Bible for a Christian's survival, especially for such a time as this and for what is yet to come. We seriously need our minds to be truly transformed by the word of God, in order that we would manifest the mind of Christ that has already been given to us as born again, spirit-filled Christians. Whether we know it or not, within the world, man's mind is constantly being manipulated and conditioned to think in certain ways and to act accordingly. Simply put, it is in a box for most and, as Christians, we are in the world and will be affected by this, except we make a wilful, deliberate effort to have our minds renewed by the word of God—to stay in it and live by it! Only then will our mind be gradually liberated from the limitations that the enemy and his agents have been, and still are, putting in the minds of men.

As a Christian, I have come to realise that our most prized possession on earth should be the WORD OF GOD! Not just in knowledge, but also in revelation and understanding with the wisdom, discernment, boldness and humility of heart to apply

The Oil

it in season! We will need to be able to live above what we see or experience which are contrary to us only by living in the word!

First Peter 13 says, 'Therefore gird up the loins of your mind [get your mind prepared], be sober and rest your hope fully upon the grace that is to be brought to you at the revelation of Jesus Christ [**through the word**]; as obedient children, **not conforming yourself to the former lust as in your ignorance;** but as he who called you is holy, you also be holy in all your conduct because it is written 'be holy, for I am holy'."

The word of God is also our spiritual food. The Lord said, in Matt.4:4, "Man shall not live by bread alone, but by every word that proceeds from the mouth of God." Just as good food is fuel for the body, so is the word of God fuel, or oil, for our spirit! Second Peter 2:2 describes how the Word is fuel for our spirit in this way, "As new born babes, desire the pure milk of the word that you may grow thereby."

The Holy Spirit began to make me see that the gift of God is without repentance, and the baptism and anointing of the Holy Spirit is a free gift of God to his children. If, a Christian totally renounces Christ without repentance, then the Holy Spirit can withdraw himself from that Christian. Also the anointing is a free gift from God, and He alone can give it to whom He will. It is not something we take at will on our own. We can only receive it from God as Christians. The Spirit and the anointing cannot be taken. They are freely given by God Himself. In the passage, the wise virgins took extra Oil (they took it by themselves out of wisdom; <u>they were not given it!</u>) The foolish virgins were also told later by the wise ones, to go <u>and buy it for themselves!</u>

We cannot take the Holy Spirit or his anointing at will. Neither can we buy them for ourselves! When Simon offered to buy the Holy Spirit and the anointing in the book of Acts, Peter cursed him because it can't be bought! It is only God who gives them as gifts and for his purpose only. We can take, or acquire, the knowledge of the WORD of God by ourselves, and we can also buy it with, or without, money! We can buy our Bibles and Christian literature that teaches us more about the word. We can pay to go to conferences to acquire more knowledge of the word and buy teaching tapes of the word. We can also acquire the true knowledge of the word by giving or exchanging our time to study it, give up ourselves, or our flesh, to yield to it and obey it. It does not just get downloaded into us, except in rare cases by the Lord himself!

We have already established by the Word of God that Lamp in this passage represents the spirit of man and we can also see that it was the duty, or responsibility, of the virgins to take the oil for themselves.

The Bible tells us to <u>work</u> out <u>our own</u> salvation with fear and trembling (Phil 2:12). As 1 Peter 2:2 says, we must desire the word in order to achieve spiritual growth. That leaves the responsibility to us, as we have already been given all we need to do to accomplish it.

All the ten virgins already had their born again spirit, which we now know that the Lamp represents, and they NEEDED to also take extra oil with them on their spiritual journey to continue fuelling their Lamps. In this case, only half of them did.

Personally, I believe this parable refers to the entire born again Christian populace. The Holy Spirit brought me to the understanding that the oil represents the WORD OF GOD! The Bible tells us, in Psalm 119:105, "your word is a lamp to my feet and a light to my path." In other words, the word of God is the TRUE light by which we continue to see as Christians after our spirit is lit up when we give our lives to Christ. (The hearing of the word of God opens our eyes and reveals our true conditions to us as sinners and, by the convicting power of the Holy Spirit, we repent and get born again. It is the same word that continues to reveal to us, the truth about ourselves, Christ and the will of God for us!). A lamp could never last long or be effective without continuous fuelling, either by oil or—in modern days—by gas, electrical power or batteries. Either way, there has to be some kind of fuelling to keep it working effectively and at its maximum power. In this passage, the oil was needed for that and, as Christians; we do not carry physical oil, just as our spirit is not physical. WE ARE TO TAKE AND CARRY THE LIVING WORD OF GOD IN OUR SPIRIT!

The Oil

We are to take the word of God for a continuous fuelling of our spirit man, which is the lamp of God! Exodus 27:20 says, "And you shall command the children of Israel that they bring you **pure <u>oil </u>of pressed olive for the light to <u>cause</u> the <u>lamp to burn continually </u>**(underline mine)." The children of Israel were to get, and bring along, the oil by themselves. They were not given it!

I remember a vision the Lord showed me some years back. I was in prayer and saw people in a room with everyone doing various things. Some were socialising, some were trying to understand where they were and what was happening around them. Some were just curious and looking around, while others were trying to look for a way out of the room and could not find a door. The room was huge and round, but above it, close to the ceiling, was an opening that looked more like a flap or trap door and, while I was observing the scene with curiosity, I suddenly saw a huge Serpent poke its head through that opening, looking down at them, and I started to panic as I knew that they were unaware of the danger above them because no one was looking up. I also noticed an expression of glee in its eyes. Don't ask me how because I just saw it in the spirit, and I also knew in the spirit that it was also checking in on them to see that they were still there; i.e., where he wanted them to be and not attempting, nor able, to get out. Even those who were looking for a door or opening did not know where one was or how to get out.

As I continued to view the scene and becoming agitated at the fact that they were oblivious of the danger above them, I intensified in prayer. I was praying in the Spirit, so much so that my jaws and cheekbones began to ache physically, and I was becoming exhausted and feeling drained until I cried out to the Holy Spirit to give me strength. As soon as I cried out, a very powerful surge welled up deep on the inside of me and, all of a sudden, the feeling of exhaustion and physical ache of my jaws and cheekbones lifted, and a renewed strength and intensity took me over. The next thing I saw was fire coming out of my mouth and going directly upwards to the Serpent, and as soon as the fire hit it, it withdrew with the speed of lightning.

The Ten Wise and Foolish Virgins (Which group do you belong)?

I felt relieved, but I was still concerned that the opening was actually some sort of flap and was not sealed and, as such, the Serpent could return. I also wondered who the people were and what they were doing there, but just before the vision caught off, I heard the voice of the Lord saying clearly, "They are born again Christians." That shook me more than the vision itself. I slowly sat up and noticed that my dress was stuck to my body because I was drenched in sweat! For days, I was disturbed about the vision and kept meditating on it and asking the Lord, "How can born again Christians who are meant to be FREE in Christ be in prison?" as I had no other word to explain the windowless and door less room.

For days I prayed, asking the Lord the same question over and over until one early Thursday morning, I suddenly heard the Lord's voice without any warning saying, "I see you are disturbed by the vision of the born again Christians that are in prison." I became instantly alert and at attention. The Lord continued saying, "It is not a physical prison; it is the prison of their mind!"

He went on to explain how, as Christians, we become born again, but most of us won't renew our minds by His word. He said, since the fall of man, every man has inherited a DOORWAY to their mind, as they inherited the Adamic sin nature. He said when Adam and Eve accepted the thought of the enemy and acted on it, they created a doorway into their mind, and every man had inherited that until Christ came and redeemed man's mind by the shedding of His blood. A crown of thorns was placed on His head that drew out blood prior to his crucifixion. Also, He was crucified on the hill of Golgotha, meaning the "place of the skull," and it is the skull that houses, or encases, the mind of a man in the physical (that was where Adam and Eve first fell—in their minds—because they yielded them to the enemy and in their hearts by allowing the enemy's word to fill it until they finally acted it out in disobedience when they accepted and acted on the thoughts the serpent suggested to them through Eve to her husband; hence, God has to give us new hearts and the mind of Christ!) I do not believe for one second that it was simply coincidental that Christ was crucified on a hill with

The Oil

that particular name. I believe it was by divine arrangement. A crown of thorns was placed on his head. God created Adam and crowned him with glory, giving him dominion over the works of his hand. Adam fell and lost that crown of glory, and man's mind became a target and doorway for the enemy's bombardment for negative and ungodly thoughts, which the Bible refers to as fiery darts.

Our mind is the major doorway to our hearts. Whatever we allow to dwell in, and take hold of, our minds will eventually filter into our hearts, and whatever filters into our hearts, we are bound to manifest in words or actions sooner or later. That is why Peter said to Sapphire and Ananias in Acts 5:3, "Why has Satan **filled** **your heart to lie** to the Holy Spirit….?" The thought first started in their minds!

The enemy and his demons know they can't touch the Blood of Jesus over your life, nor the Holy Spirit in you, but they have been around long enough to observe and understand the carnal nature of man and know they can manipulate the mind of the carnal man and the unrenewed mind of the born again Christian — if that Christian allows it, that is. As a blood-bought redeemed Christian, you have the power not to allow it!

The enemy can, and will, prevent you in every way possible from having your mind renewed by the word of God. The more you read, study, and meditate on the word of God and submit your will to obeying it, the closer you get to manifesting the mind of Christ that is already yours by right of the new birth. The enemy can lure you away from the word in so many different ways because he knows that, if you come to know and understand your TRUE identity in Christ as revealed in the word — i.e., who you truly are in Christ, he will have no power over you whatsoever, except what you give him room for.

Second Corinthians 5:17 says, "Therefore, if anyone is in Christ, he is a new creation; old things have passed away; behold all things have become new." We then NEED the manual of the new nature to know how to work the walk of this new nature successfully, and that manual is the WORD OF GOD!

Colossians 1:21-23 says, "And you who once were alienated and enemies in your mind by wicked works, yet now he has reconciled in the body of his flesh through death to present you holy and blameless, and above reproach in his sight – if indeed you CONTINUE in the faith, grounded and steadfast and are not moved away from the hope of the gospel (the word) which you heard..."

Have you ever imagined you having, and operating, the same exact type of mind that Christ had when he walked the earth? Here is the truth- you already have it, if you are born again and Spirit-filled. To manifest it, however, you need to have your mind renewed by the word of God and submit your will to obey it!

We should not have to battle over and over again with things like worry, depression, anxiety, fear, panic, judgemental attitudes, inferiority, insecurity, shame, anger, etc. — and just before you ask if it is possible to live that, the answer is yes! If we will endeavour, and take the time, to have our minds renewed by the word of God, this is certainly possible! It will not happen overnight. It will be a gradual process, but we will just have to be diligent at it!

Remember Romans 12:2? Ephesians 4:23-24 says something similar. "And be renewed in the spirit of your mind and that you put on the new man who was created according to God in true righteousness and holiness."

The truth of the matter is that demons are afraid of the born again, Spirit-filled Christian who is filled with, and totally submitted to, the word of God. The last thing the enemy wants is for you as a Christian to come into the true knowledge of who you really are in Christ. That is one of the greatest battles a Christian faces — the battle of who, or what, possesses your mind. Is it the word of God, or the words of the world?

As long as we allow ourselves to be held captive in the prison of our carnal mind (that is, our old nature before we became born again), when we have the word of God to equip us to walk out of that prison, the enemy will continue to have a doorway and possible footholds to get back into our minds.

Whoever has the mind and the heart of a man controls him, be it the enemy or the Holy Spirit, but it is up to the man to CHOOSE who he yields it to. Since, as a born again, Spirit-filled

The Oil

Christian, your new nature possesses the mind of Christ, then you must rise up and be determined and diligent to renew the mind of your old nature into the new mind of Christ that you have now inherited by virtue of the new birth! We do this by studying the word of God and yielding our wills to obey it.

We can know the will of God. It is revealed to us through our study of the word. Recall Matthew 13: 10-11, "And the disciples came and said to him, 'why do you speak to them in parables?' He answered and said to them, 'Because it has been **given to you** to know the mysteries of the kingdom of heaven, but to them it has not been given'."

Also, in Deut.29:29, it says, "The secret things belong to God, but those things which are revealed belong to us and to our children forever that we may do all the words of this law [i.e., obey the word!]."

So, when the Lord speaks to us in a parable in His word, it is because He has given to us the ability to understand it by the help of the Holy Spirit, who will reveal it to us and by the fact that we now have the mind of Christ, as it is written, to understand it! There are many deep secrets hidden in the Lord's parables if we will persevere to study them, pray for their true revelation and understanding. There are even some parables Christ explained Himself!

Since I was so disturbed about the unsealed flap above the room, the Spirit of the Lord began to give me understanding that, for as long as we are alive and in the flesh, there will always be an open doorway into our minds. That is why it does not matter how spiritually mature we become. It will not stop the devil's thoughts from attempting to invade our minds now and again, or even from bombarding it! Ephesians 6:10-18 talks about all the armour that we NEED to put on. Verses16 and 17 say, above all, to take the shield of faith (faith comes by hearing and believing the word of God!) with which we will be able to quench all (not some!) the fiery darts of the wicked one.

I believe part of those fiery darts are ungodly thoughts into, and against, our minds. Verse 17 tells us to take the helmet of salvation (a helmet protects your head, and your head houses your mind. You come under that protection at redemption and inherit the mind of Christ!) and the Sword of the Spirit, which is the word of God. The Helmet and the Sword protect and defends us from the enemy, but it also enables us to attack him. When we choose to start renewing our mind with the word and yielding our will to obey it, then we gradually start to manifest the mind of Christ that has been given to us. I believe very strongly that anyone that finally attains a totally transformed mind through studying, understanding and yielding their will to obey the word of God will be totally free from limitations. They will be able to walk in effortless freedom with God, as they will now have, and will be able to manifest, the mind of Christ that has already been given to us. You shall know the truth, and the **truth shall make you free,** as it is written!

Chapter 9

The Word and the Mind

The word of God is a two-edged Sword (Heb 4:12). It protects and defends us. It also attacks and does damage to the enemy.

As I mentioned before, Romans 12:2, says, "And do not be conformed to this world [moulded into the world's way of thinking], but be transformed by the renewing of your mind, that you may prove what is that good and acceptable and perfect will of God." If we refuse to renew our minds by the word of God, then we will be swept along, and away, with the world because, whether we know it or not, the world's way of thinking has been, is being, and will continue to be moulded into what, and how, the enemy wants people to think and believe, in contrast to God's ways and will. It is the grand plan and purpose of the enemy to get hold of the minds of men so that he can control them for his own evil purposes. That is why the Bible says the god of this world has blinded the minds of men, and he is still blinding them. It happens through schools and controlled media. If that is all you rely on for knowledge as a man, it's highly likely you are in a prison of the mind, just where the enemy of your soul - the devil - wants you, and you might not even know it. Only the true knowledge, revelations and understanding of God's word and will open the eyes of men and deliver them.

Though we are in the world, we are not of it. We are of the kingdom of Heaven as Christians, and we are expected to live from out of that same kingdom here on earth! 1 Peter 1:13 says, "Therefore gird up the loins of your mind [prepare and strengthen yourself by the word of God for the onslaught of attack that will come against your mind!], be sober and rest your hope fully upon the grace that is to be brought to you at the revelation [through the word] of Jesus Christ. In other words, be confident upon the power of grace that will be yours at the revelation of who you are and what you have in Christ.

The dictionary definition of the word GIRD is to encircle or secure with a belt or hand. To gird one's loins means to prepare and strengthen yourself for what is to come. The Bible says, in the last days, the enemy will seek to wear down the saints (Daniel 7:25, Amplified version)! I believe this will happen in their minds. Our only protection, apart from the blood of Jesus and the Holy Spirit, is the WORD OF GOD and our TOTAL SUBMISSION to it!!! Get it on the inside of you! The survival of your mind depends on it. It is the extra oil that you need to take with you to meet the Bridegroom! The Spirit, the water (i.e. the word) and the blood agree as one, according to 1 John 5:8.

The blood and the Holy Spirit have been freely given. Even the word has been freely given, but you play your part by getting it into you! It is our spiritual food, or fuel, to keep you strong and burning brightly till Christ comes. If Christ NEEDED the word to defend himself from the enemy, believe me, we NEED it too! The parable did not say the virgins didn't take extra blood or extra Holy Spirit those are freely given without any effort on our part). What they needed extra of was the oil, which is the word! You see the Bible states **that "my people perish for lack of knowledge..." (Hos 4:6).**

Isaiah 26:3 speaks of the importance of keeping our minds fixed on the word, "Thou will keep him in perfect peace whose mind is stayed on you, because he trusts in you!" We need all the peace of mind available to us in Christ through the word. **Psalm 119:165 says, "Great peace have those who love your law (the word) and nothing causes them to stumble."**

Consider the proverb, "Wise people store up knowledge..." (Prov. 10:14). The wise virgins knew, out of wisdom, to take extra oil, which is the knowledge of the word of God!) What we heard at redemption, and from various ministers, are not enough. Acquire extra for yourself before it's too late!

"It is not good for a soul to be without knowledge..." (Prov. 19:2). Ever since the Lord began to open my eyes to these things, it has caused me to wonder who determines what we learn in society (school and media), and why? In a vision the Lord showed me, the enemy was ensuring that the people were still in the prison of their carnal minds. The Bible says the enemy has blinded the minds of men, and he still is doing so. He has even lulled them to sleep and complacency, and this includes Christians! We, as Christians, however have the mind of Christ, but the only way to truly manifest that mind is to **<u>have our minds renewed by the word of God!</u>** We cannot claim to be seated with Christ in high places, far above power and principalities, and yet unable to manifest the mind of Christ from up there. The powers and principalities have been around for a long time and understand the carnal nature of man more than man himself and, as such, they are able to manipulate and control the mind of the carnal man that has not evolved by the WORD! The RENEWED MIND of the born again, blood-bought and covered, Spirit- and word-filled man is a different ballgame entirely for the enemy! That is one thing he finds difficult to handle. Hence, the Bible says, "We overcome by the blood of the lamb and the word of our testimony" – i.e., By agreeing with, submitting to and confessing the word of God!

<u>Colossians 3:16</u>
"Let the word of Christ dwell in you richly in all wisdom, teaching and admonishing one another in psalms and hymns and spiritual songs..."

<u>Hebrews 4:12</u>
"For the word of God is living and powerful, and sharper than any two-edged sword, piercing even to the division of

soul and spirit and joints and marrow and is a discerner of the thoughts and intents of the heart."

The word of God in us will discern—i.e., recognize or separate that which is of God from that which is of our flesh and the enemy. When we have the word in us, it will also rise up in our defence and give us wisdom of choice.

I remember some time back when I used to be very fearful for no apparent reason, or so I thought. Fear would just hit me from out of the blue, and my heart would begin to beat very fast, and the hairs at the nape of my neck would rise, and I would start to sweat. I did not know what to do, and I was already a born again spirit-filled Christian. I read the word, but I wasn't much good at meditating on it then. (I am still practising, even now). One day, in the evening as I was walking on the street to the shop, it hit me again from out of the blue, and I froze still right on the street. I panicked and then heard myself say, "Dear Holy Spirit, what is this?"

I heard right back, "you are being attacked by the spirit of fear." I was shocked because I did not understand that fear was a spirit nor had a spirit, despite the fact that I had read it in the Bible. I acknowledged what I read, but I had no revelation of it. As the Holy Spirit said that, my spiritual eyes popped open, and I saw what looked like a huge bat-like figure with its wings around me. I was both horrified and repulsed. I blurted out quickly, "What do I do?" The precious Holy Spirit said, "speak the word!" Just as I wondered what word to speak, I felt a bubble deep down on the inside of me rise up and, in my mind's eye, I saw the scripture that said, "For God has not given us a spirit of fear, but of power and of love and of a sound mind." (2 Tim 1:7).

The word power in that scripture triggered up another scripture that said, "Behold, I give you authority to trample on serpents and scorpions and over all the power of the enemy, and nothing shall by any means hurt you (Lk 10:19). It instantly dawned on me that I have the authority in the name of Jesus over the enemy's power to scare me. The combination of these two scriptures exploded a holy anger and boldness within me. Right in the middle of the street, I began to declare the word saying, "It is written (I love that phrase so much!), 'For God has not given me a spirit of fear, but of power and of love and of a sound mind"; therefore, I bind you foul spirit of fear in Jesus' name, and I command you to get your filthy hands off me right now, in Jesus' name!"

As I said that, the huge flap-like wings lifted off of me like lightning, and the thing just disappeared! I stood there with my eyes and mouth wide open, very surprised that the word worked just like that. Excitement flooded over me, and it was all I could do to stop myself from screaming out with joy right there in the middle of the street. It is one thing to read the word out of Christian duty. It is another thing to actually be convinced of it and act on it. I did not care if anyone was looking at me on the street. I was just very glad that I was free! All of the times that it used to attack me, I whimpered and begged the Lord to take it away, but I had the authority all the time to do it in the name of Jesus and didn't even know it! (I had it as head knowledge, but it was not a revealed knowledge until that day) Ever since then, whenever fear tried to come over me, I would just stand up straight and speak the word boldly, knowing that it dared not come near me. It has worked every single time!

Our duty is to keep our mind so renewed with the word of God, so that when an ungodly thought invades it, there will be an automatic defence and response of the word! We have the mind of Christ (1 Cor 2:16) — this is already an established spiritual truth — but we need to manifest it by renewing our minds with the word of God! If we will not renew our minds with the word of God, despite the truth that we already have the mind of Christ, as it is written, we will not be able to effectively manifest that mind of Christ within us! Christ is the word in flesh! We will simply continue to manifest the carnal mind within, since that is what we have always had, and it is the only thing we know.

The Lord told Joshua (Joshua 1:8), **"This book of the law shall not depart from your mouth** [i.e., confess in agreement with it always], **but you shall meditate on it day and night** [think about it in your mind day and night] **that you may observe to do according to all that is written in it** [i.e., the result of thinking about it day and night is that it will begin to affect and overturn the way you previously think; alter your mind set according to the word, and you will begin to respond to it by doing what it says]". **WHOEVER OR WHATEVER HAS THE MIND OF MAN CONTROLS THAT MAN**!!!] **For then you will make your way prosperous, and then you will have good success** [i.e., the result of doing what the word says is prosperity and good success!]"

The enemy has been, and will always be, after the mind of man. He attacked it in the Garden of Eden, which brought the fall of man. He tried to attack the mind of Christ, but failed woefully because Christ faithfully repeated the word of God by saying **"it is written,"** and quoting the truth of God's word that proved the enemy's wrong. He was able to speak and quote the word because He had it in Him to quote. If we don't renew our minds with the word of God and fill our hearts with it, we will have no defence against the enemy when he comes against our minds. Even Christ NEEDED the word for His defence. So why should we think that we will survive the onslaught of the enemy against our minds without the knowledge of the word of God inside of us? The days that are upon us are going to task our minds as Christians, test our faith, our knowledge of God's word, and challenge our relationship and intimacy with Him.

So many of us quote **Ephesians 2:5-6 that says we have been made alive together with Christ by grace and raised up together with him and are made to sit together in the heavenly places in Christ Jesus. Christ is seated at the right hand of the Father in the heavenly places, far above all principality and power and might and dominion and every name that is named not only in this age, but also in that which is to come. He has put all things under his feet and gave him to be head over all things to the church which is his body, the fullness of him who fills all in all.** Much as this is true, there will be a serious testing of this in us because where you are truly seated in your mind and heart will determine how you respond to the things that will be happening to, and around, you!

You see, out of the abundance of your heart, your mouth will speak, and your actions will follow! Ensure that the abundance

The Word And The Mind

of your heart will be the word of God, so that your actions and responses will also follow!

So much has already happened under our noses and before our very eyes (though most of us hardly smell or see). It is intensifying, yet most of us are very much unaware of this and have just been caught up in our own worlds and are not paying enough attention to what is happening around us! Some of us won't even read any other materials or books—even Christian literature. We rarely have time for the Bible, yet in Daniel 9:2, the great prophet wrote, "I, Daniel, understood by books." He did not just say, "I, Daniel, understood by the scripture or the Torah," but "by books," which gives me the impression that he must have read other literature that helped him to understand the time, season and the situation that Israel was in that led him to seek the face of God in fasting and prayer like he did.

Please let me make it absolutely clear that, as Christians, our most important and most reliable book is the Holy Bible. I cannot stress this enough because, without the Bible, we will have no sense of direction or guide, nor will we be able to know the ways of God or who we are in Christ, let alone how to live the Christian life. Everything we need to know to walk a successful Christian life is in the Bible. However, there are also a lot of materials by credible, God-fearing Christians who have already received revelations by the Holy Spirit to help us along the path of our spiritual growth. Nothing stops us from reading and researching other books and materials, especially if such will enhance the true knowledge and understanding of the world we live in. We will be better equipped to make informed choices and decisions, especially with the knowledge of the word of God.

TRULY THE WORD OF GOD IS AN EYE-OPENER!

I have come across some people who are not even Christians, yet they have taken the time to study the Bible better than some Christians. The only difference is that they have HEAD KNOWLEDGE while, as a Christian, it is your RIGHT BY BIRTH OF THE BLOOD OF CHRIST TO HAVE REVEALED

KNOWLEDGE! That makes a whole lot of difference! For such people, I pray that their eyes will be opened to see enough in the word so that they will surrender their lives to Christ that He will make their known knowledge of His word a REVEALED one!

The Bible says in, 1 Corinthians 2:14, "but the natural man [someone who has not given their lives over to the Lordship of Jesus; in other words, not born again] does not receive the things of the Spirit of God, for they are foolishness to him; nor can he know them, because they are **spiritually discerned.**"

Chapter 10

Our Enemy

The devil wanted to be like God. He desired to be worshiped, but the Lord's holy angels threw him and the rebelling angels out of heaven. He could not take it when God now created Man out of the DUST of the earth, in God's own image, and gave him DOMINION over all the work of His hand. The devil was part of the work of His hand! He saw his eternal damnation and knew that he never could again return to that position of glory he once had in heaven. In his evil envy, anger and frustration, he has determined not only to make man–God's special creations to be at enmity with God like himself, but also to worship him instead of God. He coveted that position so much that it cost him his place in Heaven. He still does till today. He is also determined to take as much of God's created human beings as he can with him to Hell, which he knows will be his final place of abode.

Some of the ways he does that is by capturing the minds of men through lies, deception, manipulation, intimidation, blackmail and fear. If he suddenly appeared before you, beat his chest, introduced himself, and asked you to do something, you would most likely flee. He likes to operate incognito by deceiving and manipulating men in order to control them from behind the scenes through his agents. Even his own children, he controls with fear, terror, deception, lies and blackmail. Over the years, while men have been sleeping including the Church the devil had not only sowed his tares among the wheat, but he also steadily nurtured them in evil, prepared, and slipped, them into various positions of power in order to control the world. His main desire is still to be like God, create his own evil kingdom (his kingdom can only be evil because he is already corrupted with evil, and whatever he touches or does also becomes corrupts with evil!) here on earth and make men the creation of God's hand worship him instead of God!

I have heard some people argue that Christianity is an old pagan religion that was modernised. This is because some of the things in the old testament like the Ark have already been discovered as similar to some ancient Egyptian's religious drawings. What they fail to realise however is that the Devil established all manner of religion to cause confusion, division, but most importantly, to distract and turn man away from the one true God – man's creator and the creator of the universe and all that is in it. He set up all manner of occult practises for man to worship him through. He Satan lived in Heaven a long time with God before man appeared on the scene and he knew the things that were in Heaven. After he was kicked out of Heaven because of his rebellion, he tried to establish what is in Heaven on earth, except that everything he does is corrupt and evil and whatever he touches also becomes corrupted

So when God told Moses to build the Ark, he said after telling him what to do, having shown it to Moses, "And see to it **that you make them according to the pattern which *was shown you*** on the mountain." There was no record of an Ark sitting on the mountain, so God must have permitted Moses to see into Heaven in other to see what the Ark looked like. Satan simply tried to recreate it here on earth having known about its existence, for his evil purpose hence the similarity of it appeared on the Egyptian drawings of religious rituals.

After Satan fell and realised that there was neither forgiveness nor reconciliation with God for him, he became bitterly envious of Adam and Eve, who were created from the lowliest thing–the dust of the earth. As far as he was concerned, if God would not restore him back because he disobeyed God and rebelled, he was very confident that, if he got man into the same situation and position he was now in, that would be the end of man. He had no clue about the plan of salvation–the Lamb of God that was slain before the foundation of the world! You see, we often credit the devil with too much. He is not all-knowing like God and is limited in knowledge. In fact, he stalked man and watched patiently through the years to try and understand man and why Christ, who is the eternal word from heaven, would now come down in flesh to lay his life down for man's redemption. It is a mystery even to the angels, irrespective of whether they are holy or evil. When Christ finally did appear for this mission, he still did not understand that by persecuting him unto death through his sons, he was actually fulfilling the plans of God since it was him also who initiated the fall of man in the garden in the first place. In John 8:44, it states –

"You are of your father the devil, and the desires of your father you want to do. He was a murderer from the beginning, and does not stand in the truth, because there is no truth in him. When he speaks a lie, he speaks from his own resources, for he is a liar and the father of it". Just as Pharaoh was so determined to kill Moses, the deliverer, God decided that, since he was so determined to kill him to the extent that he was wiping out innocent lives, he might as well have him and raise him until such a time that he would be grown up enough to fulfil his destiny. So Pharaoh fulfilled God's plan against himself unknowing. God often gets people to work out His plans without their being aware of it. As it is written in 1 Corinthians 2:7-8, "But we speak the wisdom of God in a mystery, the hidden wisdom which God ordained before the ages for our glory which none of the rulers of this age knew; for had they known, they would not have crucified the Lord of glory." The evil rulers of the ages have always prided themselves about the evil and secrets knowledge they have, what they lack however is the knowledge of TRUTH. If they had or have it, they would not involve themselves in evil because even the Devil they worship hates them with a passion and keeps them trapped in FEAR. They have absolutely nothing to gain except that the Devil uses them to do his dirty and evil work and when they die, they end up in hell and in unbearable perpetual torment for all eternity which is an endless span of time.

If they or the Devil really had power, then they should be able to stop themselves from dying! God is the only one who has that type of power as he is the source and infinity of all power in heaven and on earth, below the earth, in the universe and beyond it. Jesus Christ has power and authority over life and death. God however, is love. He loves his creation, but hates evil because he is a holy God.

In case you wonder why he permits evil to happen- I have heard the question many times before.

God is a God of order and integrity. He has restored power, authority and dominion back to men through Christ and all man has to do is simply believe and come to Christ to receive and manifest them. He will not override the will of any man. Any man in Christ has the power, authority and dominion to establish the will of God on earth as it is in heaven, hence the Devil is so desperate to turn men's consciousness away from God, distort men's perception of God and blind their spiritual eyes to the TRUTH of man's real identity of who he is as God's creation! His greatest tools are men, women who *choose* to yield themselves to evil and the Media! He uses the media to manipulate the minds of men and more recently, education – deliberate mis - education of the masses.

Even now, the Devil still does not know what Gods plans are besides what is already written in the Bible, so himself and his demons do eavesdrop on prophesies being released in the Church knowing that the Lord will reveal things through his prophets.

Praise the Lord, however, because he sent Jesus! Jesus came to pay the ultimate price for man's redemption by laying down his life for men to have eternal life, so that we don't have to end up in hell! Jesus has also restored the dominion, power and authority that man lost at the fall.

I have already described what Hell looks like and its location. Should you **choose** not to believe that Hell does exist and it is a very real place, at least pray to God to confirm it to you, so that you will **know** the truth for yourself. I advise that you write down the date and time you read the description of hell and its location, so that should you end up there (I pray you don't), you will remember that you read it, but chose not to believe! That choice will have nothing to do with God or the Devil. It will be YOUR SOLE RESPONSIBILTY, as it will be **your own** choice, or decision.

I know some people believe that after death, there is nothing, or that it is all bliss. **That also is deception because the Bible says, in Hebrews 9:27, "And as it is appointed for men to die once, but after this the judgment..." Even if you acquire the secret knowledge of disintegrating into light or nothingness, on that day, you will be called out of it to face your Creator. The enemy is no Creator. He only manipulates that which has already been created by contaminating it with evil, and one of the reasons why we should not fear him is because we have been told his end. Besides, the Lord Jesus has taken back that authority and restored it back to us.**

"Nevertheless I tell you the truth; It is expedient for you that I go away: for if I go not away, the Comforter will not come unto you; but if I depart, I will send him unto you. And when he is come, he will reprove [2] the world of sin, and of righteousness, and of judgment: Of sin, because they believe not on me; Of righteousness, because I go to my Father, and ye see me no more; **Of judgment, because the prince of this world is judged.**"

Luke 10: 17-20
"And the seventy returned again with joy, saying, Lord, even the devils are subject unto us through thy name. And he said unto them, I beheld Satan as lightning fall from heaven. Behold, **I give unto you power to tread on serpents and scorpions and over all [not some] the power of the enemy: and nothing shall by any means hurt you.** Notwithstanding in this rejoice not, that the spirits are subject unto you; but rather rejoice, because your names are written in heaven.

1 Corinthians 15:57-58
"But thanks be to God, who gives us the victory through our Lord Jesus Christ. Therefore, my beloved brethren, be steadfast, immovable, always abounding in the work of the Lord, knowing that your labour is not in vain in the Lord."

1 John 5:3-5 (New King James Version)
"For this is the love of God, that we keep His commandments. And His commandments are not burdensome. For whatever is born of God overcomes the world. And this is the victory that has overcome the world — our faith. Who is he who overcomes the world, but he **who believes that Jesus is the Son of God?**"

The Bible declares of the devil, in Isaiah 14:12-17:

> How you are fallen from heaven, O Lucifer, son of the morning! How you are cut down to the ground, You who weakened the nations! For you have said in your heart: "I will ascend into heaven, I will exalt my throne above the stars of God; I will also sit on the mount of the congregation on the farthest sides of the north; I will ascend above the heights of the clouds, I will be like the Most High." **Yet you [the devil] shall be brought down to Sheol, to the lowest depths of the Pit. Those who see you will gaze at you, and consider you, saying: "Is this the man who made the earth tremble, who shook kingdoms, who made the world as a wilderness and destroyed its cities, who did not open the house of his prisoners?"** The reason they will gaze and say this is because they will come to realise that fearing him was not worth it at all, most especially all of them that are in Christ. He is *like* a roaring lion,

He is not **the** Lion, but just parading about as one – in other words, an impostor

1 Peter 5:8
Be sober, be vigilant; because your adversary the devil walks about <u>like</u> **a roaring lion, seeking whom he may devour. He walks about** *like***. He is not the Lion.**

Do you notice the "I" in this passage? It was all about "SELF," and after Adam fell, all he became conscious of and focused on was "self." To date, man is still all about "self," and the devil knows that, as long as he can get you focused on "self," he has you halfway where he wants to take you! Adam became afraid not because he had disobeyed God's instruction, but because he was naked, according to his words! Also, he refused to take responsibility for his own action of disobedience, but blamed it on Eve instead, still protecting himself. The focus of Christ, however, was on you and me, and not on Himself! If it had been, He would not have gone to the cross and laid his life down for you and me to have it!

Christ said in John 12:27-31 "Now is my soul troubled; and what shall I say? Father, save me from this hour: **but for this cause came I unto this hour.** Father, glorify thy name. Then came there a voice from heaven, saying, I have both glorified it, and will glorify it again. The people therefore, that stood by, and heard it, said that it thundered: others said, 'an angel spake to him.' Jesus answered and said, 'This voice came not because of me, but for your sakes. Now is the judgment of this world: now shall the prince of this world be cast out...'."

Despite the fact that His soul was troubled, He submitted Himself to God's will and said, "but for this cause came I unto this hour."

Matthew 26:39
"And he went a little further, and fell on his face, and prayed, saying, 'O my Father, if it be possible **let this cup pass from me**: <u>**nevertheless not as I will, but as thou wilt.'**</u> –

This was where He truly died - when He laid it down by submitting His will to the Father's will, and the manifestation of this was what physically took place on the cross. As we mature in Christ, we should be able to come to the same place as He did!

"The thief [the Devil] does not come except to steal, and to kill, and to destroy. I [Jesus] have come that they may have life, and that they may have it more abundantly" (John 10:10).

For this, we NEED TO SUBMIT OURSELVES TO THE LORD AND HIS WORD TOTALLY, NOT COMPROMISING. "Submit yourselves therefore to God. Resist the devil, and he will flee from you" (James 4:7). It is after we have first submitted to God that we are told to the resist the devil, and he has no choice but to flee! The Lord Jesus, who is the author and finisher of our faith, did exactly the same thing when he was tempted of the devil. He submitted himself to God and the word and resisted the devil. The devil had no choice but to leave him alone (Luke 4:1-13)!

By ourselves, we can do nothing, but we are able to do all things through Christ, who strengthens us!

Philippians 4:13
"I can do all things through Christ who strengthens me."

One thing every true human being created in the image of God needs to understand is that, whether you are the holiest man that ever walked the face of the earth or the vilest devil worshipper that ever lived, as long as you are a human being created in the image of the one true God, the devil hates you with a passion! A passion with a capital P. So it is wisdom to seek the one true God. Even his own children and servants as well as those that worship him, he hates. He is not capable of Love. He does not have it to give. Only God and Jesus have love in such limitless abundance the Bible says in John 3:16 - For God so loved the world that He gave His only begotten Son, that whoever believes in Him should not perish but have everlasting life.

The Bible says, in Isaiah 55:6-7, "Seek the LORD while He may be found, Call upon Him while He is near. Let the wicked forsake his way and the unrighteous man his thoughts; let him return to the LORD, and He will have mercy on him and to our God, for He will abundantly pardon."

I know without a shadow of doubt that, if any man truly desires to know the one true God and the one true way He has established to reach Him and asks God to reveal the truth and the way to him, God will DEFINITELY ANSWER. Before I became a born again Christian, I was into all sorts of stuff, as there was so much confusion about which was the one true religion. I decided, on my own, to challenge God, telling him that if He is real, if He has one or more religion, or even a person dead or alive by which He can be reached, He should show me, as I truly desired to know and serve God. I also told Him that there was too much confusion and too many teachings out there, and I needed to know the TRUTH!

My grandma told me, as a child, that you reach God through idol worshiping, and I believed her and did everything with her as I loved her dearly. If my dad had not died early and I had not become separated from her, I was being primed or groomed to become an idol priestess because, according to her, I was a very strange child. My Mum told me there was a God in heaven, who created all things, and that idol worshipping was wrong, and she suffered dearly for this view, as she was labelled a witch for not participating in idol worshiping. She, however, was not sure exactly how to reach this God, but she read the book of Psalms and prayed a lot when she was going through difficulties – a practice I later adopted as I grew up. Finally, my friends introduced me to all sorts of things after I left home until I came to believe in so many different things and ways to reach God. I however got to a place where I became confused and finally fed up, so I decided to find out for myself and to stop believing everything I was told.

I also told God that, 'if He did not answer my prayer, I would conclude that He's probably not real, and He should not blame me for not serving Him if He refuses to answer me'. BUT HE DID ANSWER ME. When you know the truth, it will MAKE YOU FREE!!! You will not need anyone to tell you. You will **KNOW** WITHOUT A SHADOW OF DOUBT IN YOUR HEART

THAT GOD IS REAL, AND HE HAS SENT ME AND YOU A SAVIOUR WHO IS CHRIST JESUS WITH THE GIFT AND BLESSING OF REDEEPMTION FOR RECONCILIATION! IT IS INDEED A GLORIOUS EXPERIENCE AND WALK – A MOST EXCITING AND TRUSTING WALK INDEED! IF YOU ARE NOT YET BORN AGAIN, I CHALLENGE YOU TO TRY IT! IT'S LIKE A MASK FALLS OFF YOUR FACE, A WEIGHT IS LIFTED OFF OF YOU, AND YOU FEEL SQUEAKY CLEAN ON THE INSIDE! AT LEAST, THAT WAS MY OWN PERSONAL EXPERIENCE, AND I HAVE HAD MANY MORE GLORIOUS EXPERIENCES SINCE, AS THE LORD PERMITS.

Psalms 95:1-8 declares:

> Oh come; let us sing to the LORD! Let us shout joyfully to the Rock of our salvation. Let us come before His presence with thanksgiving; Let us shout joyfully to Him with psalms. For the LORD is the great God, **and the great King <u>above</u> all gods. (Underline, mine).** In His hand are the deep places of the earth; The heights of the hills are His also. The sea is His, for He made it; And His hands formed the dry land. Oh come, let us worship and bow down; Let us kneel before the LORD our Maker. For He is our God, and we are the people of His pasture, and the sheep of His hand. Today, if you will hear His voice: Do not harden your hearts, as in the rebellion.

I never believed in Heaven or Hell, though I had heard about them, but now I do not only believe, I **<u>KNOW</u>** THEY EXIST AS I HAVE SEEN BOTH PLACES, AND THEY ARE VERY REAL!

Chapter 11

Our Choices

The Lord also explained to me, after talking about the prison of the mind, that when He created the world, of all the planets, He chose the dust of the EARTH to make man with because man was to dwell on the earth and, as such, he would be able to adapt and live harmoniously with his natural physical environment. Since the devil was cast out of heaven and chose to come down to earth with great wrath, knowing that his time was short, the Lord gave man a roadmap and a guide to stay out of his path, complete His purpose on earth and return to Him. Besides, He even sealed this road map and guide with blood for an everlasting covenant.

I asked Him what road map this is, as I thought it was some kind of geographical map, and he answered, saying, "THE WORD"! As soon as He said the word, I saw in the open sky "THE WORD" spelt out in vapour, and I was intrigued by it. As I continued to look, I wondered why vapour? Why not in black or any legible ink, or something like that? The Lord heard my thought and said, "In your study of Geography in school, what happens to water?" I was instantly thrown off balance, so to speak, and wondered what water and geography had to do with the word? But He just carried on and said, "Be it rain or sea, river or ocean?" Suddenly, the only thing I could remember from my Geography class was that water does evaporate and gather in the clouds and, when it becomes too heavy for the atmosphere, it comes back down as rain, and I explained exactly that.

He also asked me, "What happens when we speak?" I had no clue what He meant, so I did not say anything, and He answered Himself and said, "When you speak, vapour comes out of your mouth. It is more obvious during the winter months, but anytime a man speaks, he releases vapour, whether it is visible to the naked eye or not. These vapours don't just disappear into thin air. They evaporate too and gather **in his** atmosphere, following him everywhere he goes, and when the due time comes, they fall back down upon, and into his life, just as the rain comes back down to the earth from where it started; hence, it is written that a man shall have what he says. Also, a man is snared - **trapped** by the words of *his* mouth. He is taken captive by the words of his mouth!"

He went on to say that is why Joshua was told, "Do not let this book of the law depart from **your mouth**..." That is why we are also admonished to speak in agreement with the word. It is written that we will have what we say! So, if a Christian learns, agrees and chooses to speak the word of God concerning him and in whatever situation he finds himself, in due time it will rain back upon his life. If he chooses to speak his circumstances all the time, or the devil's thoughts that come into his mind, that's exactly what will continue to manifest in his life; hence the Bible says, "**take no thought** [from the enemy]...... (Matt 6:31).

When we take and accept the devil's thoughts and continuously speak them, that's exactly what we will get! The evidence that we have taken, or accepted the devil's thoughts is in our saying them! We must repent of it, renounce the thought, and cancel them by the blood of Jesus. The Lord continued, saying except we return to His word, abide in it and let it abide in us, accepting no contrary thoughts from the enemy by speaking it, but continuously speak in agreement with His word concerning us and whatever situation we find ourselves in, we will continue to have stumbling paths ahead of us!

Joshua obeyed God's command and never allowed the word of God to depart from his mouth, and even before he was commanded thus, he already practised it. He was one of the only two spies who spoke in agreement with what the Lord had said before concerning giving them the land, and since all the elements were created by the Word of God spoken in faith, when he commanded the sun and the moon, they instantly recognised and obeyed the word of faith from his mouth! The Bible says in, **Proverbs 18:21**, "**Death** and **life** are in the **power of the tongue**, and those who love it will eat its fruit."

What most people, including Christians, do not realise is that there is a serious battle raging 24/7 for our minds. There are demons assigned to the minds of men—especially born again Christians - from the time we wake up in the morning to bedtime. They seek ways constantly to distract you from anything to do with God, be it in reading the word, meditating on it, or praying. Have you ever wondered why some unexpected and ungodly thoughts suddenly invade your mind as a Christian? If you do not know how to constantly bring such under the word of God, then you just engage yourself in a mental spiritual battle unawares by struggling to get rid of it with your willpower.

Sometimes a sudden reminder of an offence you have forgiven begins to play up in your memory, and if you don't bring it under the word, before you know it, it spills over into your emotions and, if unchecked, goes on to cause you to manifest a negative reaction. More often it's your imagination that they go for, and they keep projecting these ungodly images into your imaginations, and you wonder why you are thinking these thoughts when you really don't want to as a Christian. Those thoughts have just been projected into your mind by a demon without your awareness. As a Christian, you have the power, in the name of Jesus, to cast them down and bring them into subjection under the word of God!

Besides instead of allowing the enemy to engage your mind, there is a better way which declares in

Colossians 3: 1-3. If then you were raised with Christ, seek those things which are above, where Christ is, sitting at the right hand of God. 2 **Set your mind on things above, not on things on the earth.** 3 For you died, and your life is hidden with Christ in God.

Also Philippians 4:8 declares-[Meditate on These Things] Finally, brethren, whatever things are true, whatever things are noble, whatever things are just, whatever things are pure, whatever things are lovely, whatever things are of good report, if there is any virtue and if there is anything praiseworthy — meditate on these things.

2 Corinthians 10:5
"**Casting down** arguments and every high thing that exalts itself against the knowledge of God, bringing every thought into captivity to the obedience of Christ."

That is the word of God. For the matured Christian who has their mind renewed, it could even be distractions to do with church activities and fellow Christians - anything, as long as it is able to distract you from focusing on praying, meditating, and waiting on the Lord. Hence, it is very important to bind our minds to that of Christ and constantly bring our thoughts under the blood covering, especially for the days that are upon us.

The Lord also told me, during a visitation, that when He looks into the future of man on earth and sees what is going to happen, He sends a child into the world that will establish His (the Lord's) will for such a time as will come, and he watches over that child, bringing them to know Him, and He begins to lead them in the way that they should go. He said, however, that only a few choose to walk in the path that He lays out for them, so many become distracted by the desires of their flesh and the things of the world. Some who choose to follow Him get to the place where they have to lay it all down and, because they refuse to trust Him enough and are not willing to die to themselves, they either abandon their calling or become stagnated at a point with it and stop bearing fruit as they ought, thereby not completing their race and purpose in life.

King Solomon was prepared by God for a purpose, and he started out well. The Bible has this to say about him and his time as king.

Our Choices

Then King David rose to his feet and said, "Hear me, my brethren and my people: I had it in my heart to build a house of rest for the ark of the covenant of the LORD, and for the footstool of our God, and had made preparations to build it. But God said to me, 'You shall not build a house for My name, because you have been a man of war and have shed blood.' However the LORD God of Israel chose me above all the house of my father to be king over Israel forever, for He has chosen Judah to be the ruler. And of the house of Judah, the house of my father, and among the sons of my father, **He was pleased with me to make me king over all Israel. And of all my sons (for the LORD has given me many sons)** <u>He has chosen my son Solomon to sit on the throne of the kingdom of the LORD over Israel.</u> Now He said to me, "<u>It is your son Solomon who shall build My house and My courts; for I have chosen him to be My son, and I will be his Father. Moreover I will establish his kingdom forever, if he is steadfast to observe My commandments and My judgments, as it is this day.</u>" Now therefore, in the sight of all Israel, the assembly of the LORD, and in the hearing of our God, be careful to seek out all the commandments of the LORD your God, that you may possess this good land, and leave it as an inheritance for your children after you forever.

"As for you, my son Solomon, know the God of your father, and se<u>rve Him with a loyal heart and with a willing mind; for the LORD searches all hearts and understands all the intent of the thoughts. If you seek Him, He will be found by you; but if you forsake Him, He will cast you off forever</u>. Consider now, for the LORD has chosen you to build a house for the sanctuary; be strong, and do it."

David also prayed this for him, "And give my son Solomon a loyal heart to keep Your commandments and Your testimonies and Your statutes, to do all these things, and to build the temple for which I have made provision."

Now Solomon the son of David was strengthened in his kingdom, and the LORD his God was with him and exalted him exceedingly... And Solomon went up there to the bronze altar before the LORD, which was at the tabernacle of meeting, and offered a thousand burnt offerings on it. On that night God appeared to Solomon, and said to him, "Ask! What shall I give you?" And Solomon said to God: "You have shown great mercy to David my father, and have made me king in his place. Now, O LORD God, let Your promise to David my father be established, for You have made me king over a people like the dust of the earth in multitude. Now give me wisdom and knowledge that I may go out and come in before this people; for who can judge this great people of Yours?"

Then God said to Solomon: "Because this was *in your heart*, and you have not asked riches or wealth or honour or the life of your enemies, nor have you asked long life—but have asked wisdom and knowledge for yourself, that you may judge My people over whom I have made you king— wisdom and knowledge are granted to you; and I will give you riches and wealth and honour, such as none of the kings have had who were before you, nor shall any after you have the like." (2 Chronicles 1:1, 6-12). (Bold and italics mine)

However, see how Solomon ended his walk with the Lord:

But King Solomon loved many foreign women, as well as the daughter of Pharaoh: women of the Moabites, Ammonites, Edomites, Sidonians, and Hittites— **from the nations of whom the LORD had said to the children of Israel, "You shall not intermarry with them, nor they with you. Surely they will turn away your**

Our Choices

hearts after their gods." <u>Solomon clung to these in love</u>. And he had seven hundred wives, princesses, and three hundred concubines; and his wives turned away his heart. **For it was so, when Solomon was old, that his wives turned his heart after other gods; and his heart was not loyal to the LORD his God, as was the heart of his father David.** *For Solomon went after Ashtoreth the goddess of the Sidonians, and after Milcom the abomination of the Ammonites. Solomon did evil in the sight of the LORD, and did not fully follow the LORD, as did his father David. Then Solomon built a high place for Chemosh the abomination of Moab, on the hill that is east of Jerusalem, and for Molech the abomination of the people of Ammon. And he did likewise for all his foreign wives, who burned incense and sacrificed to their gods.*

So the LORD became angry with Solomon, because his heart had turned from the LORD God of Israel, who had appeared to him twice, and had commanded him concerning this thing, that he should not go after other gods; but he did not keep what the LORD had commanded. Therefore the LORD said to Solomon, "Because you have done this, and have not kept My covenant and My statutes, which I have commanded you, I will surely tear the kingdom away from you and give it to your servant. **Nevertheless I will not do it in your days, for the sake of your father David; I will tear it out of the hand of your son. However I will not tear away the whole kingdom; I will give one tribe to your son for the sake of My servant David, and for the sake of Jerusalem which I have chosen."** (1 Kings 1-13)

Solomon turned away from God, and he became disillusioned:

I, the Preacher, was king over Israel in Jerusalem. And I set my heart to seek and search out by wisdom concerning all that is done under heaven; this burdensome task God has given to the sons of man, by which they may be exercised. I have seen all the works that are done under the sun; and indeed, all is vanity and grasping for the wind. What is crooked cannot be made straight, and what is lacking cannot be numbered. I communed with my heart, saying, "Look, I have attained greatness, and have gained more wisdom than all who were before me in Jerusalem. My heart has understood great wisdom and knowledge." And I set my heart to know wisdom and to know madness and folly. I perceived that this also is grasping for the wind. For in much wisdom is much grief [this is not true of Godly wisdom in total submission to God]. And he who increases knowledge increases sorrow. (Ecclesiastes 1:12-18)

His father King David ended with a different state of mind, blessing God. Joshua was another example who finished well, and so was Joseph. So you see, we have a choice and whatever we choose, is what we yield our strength or will to do.

A greater number of people, though they profess to be Christians, don't even seek him, let alone discover His calling on, and His purpose for, their lives. They return to Him in thousands with their destiny unfulfilled!

Jeremiah 1:4-5 talks about his being called from the womb. Then the word of the LORD came to me, saying: Before I formed you in the womb I knew you; Before you were born I sanctified you; I ordained you a prophet to the nations."

So many prophesied births both in the Bible and today, It just goes to show that the Lord knows and ordains us before we are even born!

I need you to know that no matter how late in life you come to know or understand this, it is never too late as long as you are still alive.

In Romans 11:29, it declares-
For the gifts and the calling of God are irrevocable. It is better to do something than do nothing at all!

Our Choices

The Lord also said that, for every child He sends into the world, he put their gifting in their hands, for them to live by and bless the world with. Then again, most, rather than seeking Him to discover their gifting in the process, follow after their own understanding or the dictates and pressures of family and society and the world they live in, and they end up treating their gifts as hobbies and interests, then they end up in jobs that are not fulfilling for them.

When you discover your gift and follow after it, there is an inner passion besides yourself that drives you to excel, and you will keep reproducing, as you will never run out of ideas. It will never bore you, and where other people find it difficult to do, it will always come naturally to you. Even on occasions when you seem at a loss for ideas or know how, ask the Holy Spirit! You will be amazed at what happens! Try it and see, but ensure you do it believing!

I tell you, it is fun walking with the Lord exhilarating, I should say and when you do go through trials and temptations, for as long as you keep your focus locked on the Lord and on His word, you will always be victorious. Now when I see that the Lord permits that I go through some difficult situations, I try to look out for what I am supposed to learn from it, if anything. Besides, He always brings us out stronger. The best candidate to minister about pain is one who has gone through it!

The book of Isaiah declares that we will be perfected in the furnace of affliction. Also, since we are the spiritual descendants of Jacob, who have also inherited the Abrahamic blessings, this too is for us:

> But now, thus says the LORD, who created you, O Jacob, and He who formed you, O Israel: "Fear not, for I have redeemed you; I have called you by your name; You are Mine. **When** you pass through the waters, I will be with you; **and** through the rivers, they shall not overflow you. **When** you walk through the fire, you shall not be burned, nor shall the flame scorch you. (Isaiah 43:1-2)

This brings me to an understanding that there is a time of going through the waters, rivers, and the fire. **Matthew 3:11 says,** "I indeed baptize you with water unto repentance, but He who is coming after me is mightier than I, whose **sandals** I am not worthy to carry. He will baptize you with the Holy Spirit and **fire.**"

I know so many of us, as Christians, have been baptized with the Holy Spirit, but not many of us have been baptized with fire.

Have you ever felt overwhelmed by problems? Or feel like you are drowning under them, or feel as if your body or world is on fire and, what's more, sometimes it looks or feels like you are all alone as you are going through the storm, and it looks like there is no end in sight. Be assured, the Lord is sleeping in your boat!

Have you pondered this passage of scripture before? Mark10:29-31, "So Jesus answered and said, 'Assuredly, I say to you, there is no one who has left house or brothers or sisters or father or mother or wife or children or lands, for My sake and the gospel's, who shall not receive a hundredfold now in this time houses and brothers and sisters and mothers and children and lands, **with persecutions** and in the age to come, eternal life. But many who are first will be last and the last first'."

So many of us like to claim the hundredfold houses, brothers and sisters and mothers and children and lands, but never the persecutions, forgetting that it's part of the package!

Some of us start to go through it and abort the process because we simply are not willing to die to self. Only a few will go all the way, trusting the Lord and His word to see them through it. Fire both ignites and purifies, and most of us are not that willing to begin to die to self and submit in total surrender to God and his will.

Consider the many mentions of persecution in the Bible.

Matthew 5:10
"Blessed are those who are **persecuted** for righteousness' sake, for theirs is the kingdom of heaven."

Matthew 5:12
"Rejoice and be exceedingly glad, for great is your reward in heaven, for so they **persecuted** the prophets who were before you."

John 15:20
"Remember the word that I said to you, 'A servant is not greater than his master.' If they **persecuted** Me, they will also persecute you. If they kept My word, they will keep yours also."

However sometimes what may seem like extreme persecution is just a test of faith, like when Abraham was commanded to kill Isaac his only son—the son of God's promise. The Lord told the house of Israel that He has tested them in the furnace of affliction. "Behold, I have refined you, but not as silver; I have **tested** you in the furnace of affliction" (Is 48:9-11).

Exodus 16:4
"Then the LORD said to Moses, "Behold, I will rain bread from heaven for you. And the people shall go out and gather a certain quota every day, that I may **test** them, whether they will walk in My law or not."

Deuteronomy 8:16
"Who fed you in the wilderness with manna, which your fathers did not know, that He might humble you and that He might **test** you, to do you good in the end?"

Judges 3:4
And they were left, that He might **test** Israel by them, to know whether they would obey the commandments of the LORD, which He had commanded their fathers by the hand of Moses."

Jeremiah 17:10
"I, the LORD, search the heart, I **test** the mind, Even to give every man according to his ways, According to the fruit of his doings."

Jeremiah 20:12
"But, O LORD of hosts, You who **test** the righteous, And see the mind and heart, Let me see Your vengeance on them; For I have pleaded my cause before You."

So sometimes, it's just a test! Be it a test or a persecuting trial, the important thing is for us to totally TRUST God and KNOW that we are safe in His hands!

Chapter 12

Trusting the Lord

I remember once, when I was going through a very rough period, I felt as if I was spinning in a void and did not know what else to do, but to trust God totally and believe that He would see me through. I cried out to God in prayer one day, as per my usual custom, and I saw a vision. I saw a very bad storm in the midst of the sea, and I noticed that someone was in it without a boat or any covering, and this person was being tossed up and down violently by the waves. I peered at this person and realised it was me! I expected to drown and die any minute, as I don't swim, and there was no help in sight. As I continued to watch, I saw that I was just getting tossed about violently and was not drowning. I began to wonder why I was still afloat in the situation, considering the fact that I was helpless against it. The Lord opened my eyes further, and I noticed that, from my chest cavity, was a long silver cord, stretching all the way into the heavens, and as I wondered what that was and where it was going, I saw the word "HOPE" written on it. Then I heard the Lord speak, "For as long as your hope is in Me, you cannot sink. The sea of trials may toss you to and fro as much as it likes, but it won't drown you because your hope is anchored in Me and, for as long as your hope is anchored to Me, no trial can take you under. Should it attempt to, I will bring you back up and out!"

That was the day I fully understood the power of trusting and hoping in the Lord!

Another time, one of my brothers was deported back to Africa from a foreign country where he had sojourned for five years. The family was downcast about the situation, and I decided to pray, as I felt very overwhelmed by the situation. I asked the Lord why He let this happen. As I stayed on my knees in prayer, I saw myself wearing all black in mourning attire and sitting on a lone bench at the airport, and people came paying their condolences asking what, or whom, I was waiting for? I told them I was waiting for my brother's corpse to take it home for burial. I finally boarded the plane and saw a coffin being loaded on. As it came up on its way to the cargo hold, the cover fell off, and I saw it was empty. I jumped up, shouting, "Where is my brother's corpse? Who has taken his body away?" Suddenly, I came back to myself, realising that I was still on my knees inside the room and had just been in a trance.

I was badly shaken, since the same brother was the one who had been deported and was sitting down in the front room. Then the Lord spoke and said, "If I had not allowed them to deport him home, that is how you would have received him - in a casket". I jumped up and started to furiously thank God for the deportation, and when I told the other members of the family, they also changed and started to thank God for the situation! Sometimes, we don't just know, but God knows it all! My brother was the family's black sheep then. He is out of the country again now, as the Lord took him back out, but he is a different person, as he is now fully born again and serving God.

So, oftentimes, we have no clue what is happening behind the scenes on our behalf. We just judge what we see in the physical, but the Lord knows and sees all things; hence, we have to learn to trust Him totally!

I've mentioned that "It is written" is my favourite phrase in the entire Bible. There is a sense of authority and finality about it. All the time the devil tempted Jesus, He responded with, "It is written". There is nothing the enemy can do with the written word!

The Lord also says, in the book of Isaiah (55:11), "so shall my word be that goes forth from my mouth, it shall not return to me void, but shall accomplish that which I please and prosper in the thing for which I sent it."

Further, the Lord tells us, "I watch over my word to fulfil it (Jer. 1:12). "...The Lord has magnified his word above all his name..." (Ps 138:2).

He is not a man to lie, or the son of man to repent of His word. If He says it, He will bring it to pass.

The same three temptations that the devil gave to Eve that Adam followed were also given to Jesus. - The lust of the flesh, eyes and the pride of life. All three temptations are what still revolve around man today in various forms!

First John 2:16 says it is all that is in the world. The enemy just presents them in various forms and packaging, depending on which one or type will attract your lust and mine. The same way the Lord responded by saying, "it is written" is how we should also respond at all times no matter what, but this can only be achieved if we have the word already resident and rooted on the inside of us! We cannot give what we do not have, and it is the word of God that we have on the inside of us that the Holy Spirit will quicken to us in the instant that we need it!

We also have to learn to agree with the word and the revelation of it by the Holy Spirit, whether it makes sense to us or not. The Bible says, in Amos 3:3, "How can two walk together except they agree?" When we learn to agree with the word of God, confessing it, choosing and being diligent to obey it, we soon begin to see the manifestation of it in our lives. Even in the face of temptations and trials, when we yield to the word instead of the situation, we receive grace to go through it. "When you pass through the waters, I will be with you and through the rivers, they shall not overflow you when you walk through the fire, you shall not be burned nor shall the flame scorch you" (Isaiah 43:2). WE NEED TO HAVE THE WORD IN US TO OVERFLOWING! Until it becomes the only thing that flows from us automatically in response to confronting situations in our daily lives and the Spirit of the Lord will bring them into manifestation, just like when the empty clay pot was **filled to the brim** with water [the

The Ten Wise and Foolish Virgins (Which group do you belong)?

word] and, on drawing it out, it had transformed to wine, a manifestation of the Spirit!

This passage in Isaiah says WHEN, and not IF. This tells me that there will be period in our lives when we will have to go through water and fire as I earlier mentioned! I am not writing this because I am any better than the next person at walking through trials. I am writing this because I have come to understand it and am determined, and am praying all the time to achieve the ultimate victory over my trials, by His grace and the keeping power of His word. Sometimes we are refined in the fire of affliction, but we come out purified, ignited and ablaze, not burnt in preparation for more of the Lord's glory.

On one of the very rare occasions that the Lord has permitted me to come up before His throne room, He showed me things that I cannot write about now, nor am I hardly able to talk about. He also showed me later, during the same visitation, the effect of his purifying fire upon the life of a Christian, and the result was astounding and very glorious. I came back from that experience pondering the things I had seen. A few days later, I walked into a prayer meeting for the first time, and I was not even there for five minutes when the leader suddenly walked up to me and nudged me by the elbow, asking me to pray. I was very surprised since I knew no one there, and it was my very first visit. Even the lady who had invited me was not around. Since I was not sure what they were praying about before I walked in, I just asked the Holy Spirit quietly to help me pray, which is my usual habit.

As soon as I said that, one of the scenes I had seen in the throne room flashed before me, and I began to pray that the Lord would send his cleansing, purifying fire down upon us. I was not exactly sure what I expected, but all of a sudden, I heard a sudden switching explosive, but gentle, noise, and it was as if everyone was simultaneously caught up and ignited, as the whole atmosphere became electrifying, and there was a sudden and serious explosion of praying going up. After the prayer meeting ended, the leader's wife came up to me, introduced herself, and told me I was an intercessor. I had no clue what she was on about, as that was my first time hearing such a word.

The short of it all is that, after some time, I began to go through a very difficult and trying period in my life. It was as if everything was falling apart in my life, and it was very uncomfortable for me. It got so bad that, one day, I lifted up my face to heaven and cried out to God, asking Him what kind of a Father are you that you will let me go through this. Please understand that, despite my spiritual experiences, I had not really grown up spiritually then, neither am I fully grown now. I am still growing, although I have come a long way since then.

On two separate occasions, I went through similar experiences and reacted exactly the same way – like a spoilt brat throwing a tantrum. A few years later, as I was asking the Lord to cleanse and purify me, He spoke gently and said, "you have asked for these before, and twice I have sent my cleansing fire, but you were not willing to bear it. You even asked me what kind of a Father I am." I was very shocked when both periods flashed before me, and I felt very foolish for having reacted the way I did. What I needed to do was TRUST Him and rely on His GRACE and the keeping power of His WORD! My spirit was willing, but my flesh was weak, and the self in me was not willing to die!

Not until we come to the place where we become willing to lay it all down and start dying to self, we will not truly begin to live!

The word of God will bring us deliverance, cleansing, healing, freedom, peace, confidence and strength, and much more in our time of need!

I have often heard Christians quote the scripture that says, "There is therefore now no condemnation to those who are in Christ Jesus", but that is not all of this particular scripture. It goes on to say, "<u>who do not walk according to the flesh; but according to the Spirit.</u>" Some of us take the word and the things of God for granted, not realising that it is to our own detriment. We abuse the grace of God over and upon our lives, and I have often heard some Christians say we can't do anything of ourselves, but only by grace, which is true—without

The Ten Wise and Foolish Virgins (Which group do you belong)?

Christ, we can do nothing. We, however, have to be willing to submit our wills to obey God, and then the power of grace comes to enable us! The grace of God does not override a man's will! It enables, or empowers, him after he chooses to yield his will in obedience to God!

One time, when I was at prayer, the Lord gave me a vision. In this vision, I saw a man I recognised as having seen on TV before. I believe he was a minister of the word. In the vision, he was sitting at his desk in his church office, and I heard him enquire from a lady about some carpentry work that needed doing and had previously been contracted out to a man. For whatever reason, however, this contractor did not complete the work, and this angered this man of God. He chose to go and sort it out with the contractor himself. As the contractor saw him coming, he quickly ducked into a house, trying to avoid this man of God, but the man of God went in after him and was suddenly confronted by a stark naked beautiful woman. The man of God stopped dead in his tracks, staring at this naked woman in front of him (the contractor was out of the scene by now).

I could see that he was becoming physically aroused at the sight confronting him, and I turned to look at the Lord, who was standing a short distance from me, but He told me to look at the scene, so I turned back again to see what this man of God would do. All of a sudden, as he continued to stare at the woman, I could see that all his physical senses were being aroused and pulled towards what his gaze was fixed upon, and the woman in question made no attempt to cover herself up (I also knew, in the spirit, that she was a member of his congregation); rather, she was giving this man of God a very sultry come-on look. At the same time, the scriptures began to pop up on the inside of him pertaining to sin and fleeing sexual immorality. At the popping up of the scriptures, he suddenly stood straight and CHOSE to yield all his strength [will] to the word of God that had risen up on the inside him, and he **RESOLVED IN HIMSELF** THAT HE WOULD NOT SIN AGAINST GOD!

As soon as he did that, I saw what looked like a transparent glass shaft drop from heaven upon him, and a sudden holy anger welled up on the inside of him. Some sort of strength came over him, and he stormed out of the house. Then the Lord turned to me and said, "Did you see that nothing happened to him until he resolved in himself to obey the word of God?" And I asked what the glasslike shaft was, and He said that was the empowering strength of grace, but did I notice that it did not come upon him until he **chose to obey** the word? Only then did he receive grace and strength to truly stay out of sin. I then asked the Lord what would have happened if he had gone the way of the dictates of his flesh. He replied that, despite the availability of grace, he would have fallen into sin! The Lord explained that the grace of God is always available to us, all we need to do is yield ourselves to the word, and the grace will automatically become available to us in time of need. Despite the free availability of grace, it will not override the will of man. Neither will the word of God, God Himself, nor the Holy Spirit! Man has to be willing to yield his will, and then the Lord gives him the strength, or power, of grace to obey and do the thing he ought or need to do.

When we choose to submit to God and His word instead of the dictates of our flesh, the empowering power of grace will strengthen us, and the keeping power of the word will lead and see us through.

So, every born again, Spirit-filled Christian NEEDS to FILL THEMSELVES UP WITH THE WORD OF GOD!

We should make a habit of not just READING the word, but STUDYING IT as much as we can until it becomes REVEALED KNOWLEDGE in us. We also NEED to MEDITATE upon it because it is in the MEDITATION of the word that REVELATION comes! Revelation will bring us better UNDERSTANDING of the word. Understanding will bring us WISDOM. Wisdom will teach us the fear of the Lord, and the fear of the Lord will lead us into HUMILTY and OBEDIENCE. This will cause us to begin to LOVE in truth.

One night, I sat up studying the word till the early hours of the morning, as I was enjoying it so much and did not want to go to bed. After a while, I began to taste honey in my mouth. I was puzzled; as I knew I had not eaten any honey and did not even have any in the house. The taste began to get stronger in my mouth as I continued to study the word, until finally I realised something was going on. I stopped and I said, "Precious Holy Spirit, what is going on? Why do I taste honey so strongly in my mouth when I know I have not eaten any?" He gave me "Psalm 19:10 and 119: 103," and I opened to it straight away. It reads, "More to be desired are they [God's words] than gold. Yea than much fine gold; sweeter also than honey and the honey comb."

Psalm 119:103
How sweet are Your words to my taste, Sweeter than honey to my mouth!

I became very amazed, as I had read that scripture before and never knew it was real. I thought it was just a figure of speech. Also, sometimes you are studying the word and meditating on it so much, and you begin to smell the most beautiful fragrance ever, and you simply don't want it to stop, and you know you have company! TRUST ME. IT IS FUN AND GLORIOUS, OFTENTIMES JUST ABIDING IN THE WORD!!

Constantly studying and meditating upon the word, and submitting ourselves to obey it in our love for God, the fear of the Lord and in humility will enable us to start manifesting the fruits of the Holy Spirit. Our pastors and ministers cannot study the word for our spiritual growth. They study and teach us all right, but we have to study it for ourselves to get a personal revelation and understanding of it. That is when it becomes ROOTED in us and becomes unshakeable, except when we choose by ourselves to let go of it.

We must let the word of God dwell richly in us and allow it prepare us for his return.

Chapter 13

Preparation

"While the bridegroom was delayed, they all slumbered and slept and at midnight, a cry was heard 'behold the bridegroom is coming, go out and meet him" (Matt 25:5-6).

The Bible teaches us that no man knows the day or the hour when the Lord will return. The Lord Jesus himself said, in Matthew 24:36, "But of that day and hour, no one knows, not even the Angels of heaven, but my Father only." He, however, gives us signs of what the times will look like in the gospels, and there is no doubt in my mind that we are already in the times He spoke of. I have yet to meet a Christian who does not agree that we have indeed entered the end times. Bible prophecies are coming to pass right before our very eyes.

Second Thessalonians 2:1-12 states:

> Now, brethren, concerning the coming of our Lord Jesus Christ and our gathering together to Him, we ask you, not to be soon shaken in mind or troubled, either by spirit or by word or by letter, as if from us, as though the day of Christ had come. Let no one deceive you by any means; for *that Day will not come* unless the falling away comes first, and the man of sin is revealed, the son of per-

dition, who opposes and exalts himself above all that is called God or that is worshiped, so that he sits as God in the temple of God, showing himself that he is God.
Do you not remember that when I was still with you I told you these things? And now you know what is restraining, that he may be revealed in his own time. For the mystery of lawlessness is already at work; only He who now restrains *will do so* until He is taken out of the way. And then the lawless one will be revealed whom the Lord will consume with the breath of His mouth and destroy with the brightness of His coming. The coming of the *lawless one* is according to the working of Satan, with all power, signs, and lying wonders, and with all unrighteous deception among those who perish, because they did not receive the love of the truth, that they might be saved. And for this reason God will send them strong delusion that they should believe the lie that they all may be condemned who did not believe the truth but had pleasure in unrighteousness.

The angels that gather are already at work separating the Tares from the Wheat, according to Matt.13:24-30 and 37-43. Men have indeed been sleeping, particularly the Church. The Church is just beginning to stir and starting to sit up and among those that are coming to see, or realise, what has happened. There are not many who are sure what to do about it. Some prefer to hide their heads in the sand, like they can wish it or pray it away, and a few are speaking out like lone voices crying out in the wilderness.

Some also are afraid of persecution and would rather play it safe to keep their place, while others are pushing themselves to extremities, trying to seek the things that are to be added for free, rather than seek first the kingdom of God and being established in His righteousness, seeing they are already in the kingdom. Whichever position we take will not stop the word and will of God from coming to pass. The enemy is attacking the minds of men, including Christians, with fear of the future. We as Christians are not to be afraid because we

Preparation

---

have not been given the spirit of fear, but of love, power and a sound mind. Besides, we have the mind of Christ and are meant to manifest it.

We cannot manifest the mind of Christ, however, if we are not transforming our minds with the word of God. Christ is the manifested word of God. The transformation of our minds with the word of God is what will enable us to manifest the mind that Christ has restored back to us. The Lord told me some time back that He is looking for distributors, and as I wondered what He meant by distributors, He continued by saying He is looking for those who will align themselves with His will and His word that He may distribute wealth through them. He needs those who will have a heart for souls, for the poor, the needy and the abandoned - the widows and the fatherless, and the orphans — that He may distribute wealth through them.

He said He often releases blessings to His children to test their hearts, and most of them begin to hoard them, and they become stagnated even before they have received much. He said He created the earth and knows where her hidden wealth is, and He is searching and testing the hearts of His people to see who He can trust to distribute His wealth, as He is getting ready to do a quick work on earth.

In Proverbs 8:15-21, it says, "by me kings reign and rulers decree justice. By me Princes rule and nobles, all the judges of the earth. *I love those who love me, and those who seek me diligently will find me.* **Riches and honour are with me, enduring riches and righteousness**. My fruit is better than gold, yes than fine gold and my revenue than choice silver. *I traverse [walk about] the way of righteousness in the midst of the path of justice* **_that I may cause those who love me to inherit wealth, that I may fill their treasuries._**

Wisdom, here, is the word of God. Study the whole of Proverbs 8 and meditate on it until revelation dawns. If we will bring ourselves under the discipline of the word and will of God, determine in our hearts to TRULY walk with Him by DYING to self and yielding our will to obey His word instead of yielding to self, we will see a quick turnaround for the better in our lives.

The Ten Wise and Foolish Virgins (Which group do you belong)?

Later, in that same chapter, are these words, "Now therefore, listen to me my children, for blessed are those who keep my ways [Obedience)]. Hear instruction [the word], and be wise and do not disdain it. Blessed is the man who listens [pays attention and hears my word] to me, watching daily at my gates [studying my word daily], waiting at the post of my doors [meditating on my word]. For whoever finds me finds life and obtains favour from the Lord. But he who sins against me wrongs his own soul [we do ourselves no good by walking in disobedience to the word]. All those who hate me love death." (Words in bracket, mine)

Recently, when the Lord was talking to me about the state of the Church and the days ahead, I kept saying to myself that these messages would not be popular, compared to the messages of prosperity that are spilling out of a lot of pulpits, and that I might be labelled a scaremonger. Finally, after some time, I was walking down a hill when I suddenly felt the Lord's presence before I heard His voice and He said, "I have not called you to a popularity contest."

I was taken aback at the statement because my mind went straight to beauty pageants and contexts, but He continued and said, "The messages I have been giving you, you keep saying they will not be popular. Whatever I tell you, declare it boldly and do not be afraid, nor look at their faces. The trouble with many of my servants is that they are not willing to die. My word says whoever desires to come after me, let him deny himself, and take up his cross and follow me" Luke adds the word DAILY) to his version. He continued and said, 'The trouble is that many who claim to follow me are not willing to die. They are very mindful of their name, their image and their desires. Anyone who is not willing to lose his name for my namesake is not worthy of me, and anyone who is not ready to lose his image to take up mine is not worthy of me. My cross represents death. It is the place of crucifixion. As you carry it in your daily walk with me, you should be willing to lay it down and die whenever the need arises for death to self, but many are not willing and, as such, they become stagnated in their ministries.

Except a man is willing to die to self, he cannot truly begin to live in me nor accomplish much".

At these words, I was reminded of Matthew 16:24-25, "Then Jesus said to His disciples, 'if anyone desires to come after me, let him deny himself, and **take** up his **cross**, and follow me. ...Whoever loses his life for my sake and the gospels will find it'."

It is better to submit to death of self under grace than under persecution or trials. Grace will empower you, but persecution will likely break you, depending on your spiritual level.

Much as it is true that, by ourselves, we can do nothing and we are able to do all things through Christ who strengthens us, that does not mean that Christ Himself will override our will, nor will grace. We have the power to yield our will to whomever, or whatever, we choose.

Like I wrote earlier, when we CHOOSE to YEILD our will to obey God's word, grace empowers us to do it. Grace does not force us, nor does it override our wills. We have to be willing and choose to obey the word of God for the power of grace to become available to us. For us to continue to go through life in our Christian walk, not making efforts to grow, nor obeying God and just waiting for the time when we will start to automatically obey because grace has now taken over our wills is the greatest deception ever. God has not created robots; neither does He override anyone's will. If he did, no one would go to hell because it is not His will that anyone perish.

I heard about a young lady who was recently born again and had a pastor tell her that, because we are under grace, he could go to bed with her, and it would not be counted against them as sin because they were under grace! I could not believe my ears, though I did not know much about the scripture then, and I am still learning now, but I have the Holy Spirit and instinctively knew that to be wrong.

Division in the Body of Christ. I had no intention whatsoever to include this next section in this book, but for two days solid, the Lord has impressed it in my spirit to write it until I have come to conclude that it must be on His heart to address. This is also buttressed by my recollection of the fact that not too long ago, during intercessory prayer for the body of Christ, I suddenly went into very deep grief in my heart that I knew had nothing to do with me, as I started to pray and come against the division in the body of Christ.

After being in that grieving state for a while, I felt as if my heart had completely turned liquid and was slowly sipping out. The sensation felt very strange, but very real, and I started to feel my body to see if I was bleeding and wet. To my surprise, I felt nothing in the physical. I had never experienced anything like it before, except on that fateful day when the Lord laid a burden of grief on my heart for the division in His body.

When I finished, I began to meditate in the following days upon the things the Lord had impressed on my heart and what I had heard myself interpret during the praying session and also what He made me understand.

I believe that every serious born again Christian who is watching and praying like the Lord commanded us to in **Luke 21:36** ("**Watch** therefore, and **pray** always that you may be counted worthy to *escape* all these things that will come to pass, and to stand before the Son of Man.") will acknowledge the fact that we have entered into the end times. The Lord will take *His Church* out of the church. Whether we like to accept that as fact or not, the present-day church has been infiltrated a long time ago and is still being infiltrated. We have wolves in sheep's clothing amongst us.

Matthew 7:15 says, "Beware of false prophets, who come to you in **sheep's clothing**, but inwardly they are ravenous **wolves."** We'll know them by their fruits.

The Lord went on to say that it takes a born again Christian who is grounded in the word and has the Holy Spirit to discern good and evil. Good fruits from bad fruits and to also discern a wolf in sheep's clothing.

I joined a small local church once whose leaders truly love God. As I live close by to the church building, I offered to relieve the pastor the trouble of coming out on Sunday mornings to prepare the rented hall for service as I noticed none of the other

Preparation

members were coming to do it. When I go out to arrange the hall for service, I also take about an hour to pray for the service on that day before going home to get ready and come back for service. A visiting minister was invited once to preach, and he preached his guts out, emphasising all the miraculous happenings in his church in his home country. He started laying hands on everyone, including the ministers. Some were falling down, and there was a lot of hype.

I always like to stay at the back of the church, just quietly interceding often, as the Holy Spirit prompts me. As I listened to this minister preach, I noticed that my spirit began to grieve for no apparent reason against him, and I started to silently berate myself for daring to feel like that towards a man of God. It was becoming a distraction for me, as I was trying to fight off this grief and quietly intercede at the same time. It finally dawned on me on the inside that something was not right, but I could not tell what it was.

He finally laid hands on every single person in the congregation except me because I refused to go forward and resolved that I wouldn't let him touch me, even if he came to me. I felt quite odd, but I knew enough to follow my spirit. When he was done, he gave a prophecy concerning the Church, claiming God was speaking, that what he said was to happen in exactly three months from that day. The Church began to prepare for the manifestation of this prophecy. The next service after this particular one, I had gone again to church, as usual, and just as the reading of the word was about to start, I heard, "Go up front and pray".

Immediately I doubted that it was the Lord, as I knew I was not to interrupt the reading of the word. Besides, I had prayed for one hour earlier. At the same time, I reasoned if the enemy would ask me to go out and pray, and I decided I couldn't be hearing right. It must have been my flesh. A few minutes passed, and I heard exactly the same words. This time I told myself that this was the Holy Spirit, but He would not ask me to disrupt the reading of the word by asking me to go out and pray just before the service began and as the minister started to read the word, so it did not make sense to me. I hesitated, very reluctant to go

The Ten Wise and Foolish Virgins (Which group do you belong)?

out, not knowing what to tell the minister, who was just beginning to read the word.

The third time I heard very strongly, "go out and pray!" I said, "but Lord..." And that was as far as I uttered. I suddenly felt a gentle, but very firm, whirlwind fall upon me like a cyclone. It spun me around on my heels, and my back was now facing the pulpit. It carried me, walking backwards, all the way to the pulpit from the back of the church. (It was an average-sized hall) I did not follow a straight aisle, yet I did not hit any chair on the way.

When I got to the pulpit, it was knocked over, and so was I, lying back on the floor, and I went into one of the deepest intercession/warfare prayers I had ever been led into. I was a while on the floor, and everyone automatically began to pray in the spirit when they saw what happened. When I was done praying, and I stood up, my clothes were stuck to my body in sweat, and I felt embarrassed as I felt I had disturbed the service, but I knew what happened was totally out of my control. When I finally regained my composure, I asked the Lord what just happened, and why? He said, "I will not allow my word to be preached from a defiled pulpit."

I said, "Defiled?" as I did not understand and he explained that the last minister that came to minister there had defiled it. He showed me the face of this particular minister and another one who was there during the midweek service that I did not attend. I was shocked! I said, "Lord, I knew I was not comfortable in my spirit with the minister, but he did sound genuine. Besides, he gave a prophecy from you that is to come to pass in three months." And the Lord replied, "I did not send him. He is not of me, and the prophecy will not come to pass because I did not send him." I stood there in stunned silence and did not know how to tell the pastor, as I observed that the church ministers held him (the minister that visited) in high esteem. I began to pray and, at the end of three months, **nothing** happened, and it depressed the pastor, who had gone out of his way to prepare for the fulfilling of this prophecy.

Then the Lord asked me to tell the pastor that he should not distress himself because the prophecy did not come from Him in the first place. It took me two whole weeks to summon up the courage to tell the pastor, and he looked at me and said, "I know now because the Lord asked a sister from the US to call me and tell me exactly what you are saying last week, so I am okay, now as I was concerned, thinking I had probably not prepared well enough." And I felt such great relief.

The reason I write this is because the Lord laid it on my heart to recount the incident, but that is just to show that, sometimes, you just never know until the Lord reveals something to you! To date, apart from what I picked out concerning that false prophet in the spirit, there is no way I could have concluded otherwise about him. To this day, I do not know why the Lord showed me that second minister who defiled the pulpit.

Another occasion, I was again interceding for the body of Christ when I saw a popular TV minister with what looked like a swarm of huge, grey/black flies hovering over his head and following him everywhere he went. I recoiled from the sight and exclaimed, "Lord, what is this?" And I heard, "Spiritually, he stinks!" I was horrified and pondered how a Christian especially a minister can stink spiritually, as I had never heard such phrase before. I pondered this for days and was deeply disturbed by the sight, as I know members of his congregation. Finally, I confided in one of his ministers what the Lord had shown me concerning the head of this ministry, and he opened up and told me some serious issues with him. (He said it not out of gossip, but concern and grief, as he is a praying man too). And I understood why he stank spiritually. I was deeply saddened and started to pray for him.

Oftentimes it takes the Lord to tell, or show, us for us to see something or discern it. It can also sometimes depend on our level of spiritual maturity and gifting. I know that these two ministers still minister in churches. Sometimes, you just can't tell; hence, it is important to stay in the word and stay sensitive to the Holy Spirit.

Chapter 14

Abiding in Love

The Lord says, in **John 10:27**, "My **sheep hear my voice**, and I know them, and they follow Me." We will come to recognize, know, and hear His voice by knowing His word and being in intimate fellowship with Him!

Different denominations have their own ways of doing things, and some even have their doctrines that conflict with other denominational doctrines, and these cause division. There is no division in Christ, His blood, His Spirit, or His word. So, whatever division there is in the body of Christ is either of the enemy or manmade. The Bible says to test the spirit, and the Lord Jesus also admonished his disciples to beware of the leaven (teachings) of the Pharisees. We cannot, as Christians, test the spirit if we are not in intimate fellowship with the Holy Spirit, neither can we be able to beware of the leaven of the Pharisee if we do not have the true knowledge of the word of God. The fact that we do not see eye to eye on interpreting doctrines does not gives us the right to attack, or condemn, each other! When we do that, what we are doing is joining with the enemy to do his job for him, as he knows that there is power in unity. Any real Christian knows that the word of God can never contradict itself. It is our lack of true revelation and understanding of it, and our heart of pride, that make us believe that what we have, or that what we believe of it, must be the only correct one, not taking into account, in humility, that we may be wrong and that we should ask the Holy Spirit to reveal more or confirm it to us and, as such, whatever else we come across and do not understand, we automatically condemn.

All my growing Christian life, I have always understood the passage - that says in **Matthew 16:19**, "And I will give you the keys of the kingdom of heaven, and **whatever** you **bind** on **earth** will be bound in heaven, and **whatever** you loose on **earth** will be loosed in heaven."- to mean that I could bind anything I did not want, and anything that I believe is of the Devil. At least, I used to think this way until I read *Shattering Your Strongholds* by Liberty S. Savard. Then I understood that binding is not just for negativity. It can be used positively, as well. Her teaching from the revelation she got from the Lord in that book did not contradict the word or what the church had only thought it to be. Instead, it expanded the revelation and understanding of that scripture.

I remember another occasion when I was invited to minister at a women's conference. What the Lord laid on my heart to teach needed the scripture in **Isaiah 11:2**, "The **Spirit** of the LORD shall rest upon Him, The **Spirit** of **wisdom** and **understanding**, The **Spirit** of counsel and might, The **Spirit** of knowledge and of the fear of the LORD." I began to ask the Holy Spirit exactly what the Spirit of the Lord meant here (I am aware the Holy Spirit is the Spirit of the Lord himself). The Holy Spirit said, "LOVE. GOD IS LOVE." So, for what I needed to minister, I taught it as LOVE, just as he told me to.

To my surprise, the conference leader also used the same scripture the next day, but now interpreted that same passage the Holy Spirit told me was love as "DOMINION" - THE SPIRIT OF DOMINION. As soon as I heard that, I automatically responded and said, "that can't be" because of what the Holy Spirit had earlier told me. Almost immediately, I reprimanded myself, knowing that the woman would not preach or teach what she had not heard from God, either. So I said, "Precious Holy Spirit, you are not the author of confusion. Please explain to me why you told me LOVE, and this woman DOMINION, as I know she won't teach it except by revelation from you."

The Holy Spirit replied and said, "What manner of Spirit dominates?" I thought for a few seconds and said, "You cannot dominate what you have not conquered, so it has to be a conquering Spirit." Then he said, "And what it is that conquers all?" Understanding dawned, as I remembered 1 Corinthians 13, "love conquers all!" So, you see, if I had not corrected myself quickly and taken it back to the Holy Spirit, who is our teacher, subtle pride could have taken root and caused me to claim I was the one with the real revelation, not her. Neither will I be surprised tomorrow if the Lord reveals more on it. He is able to give various meanings to one scripture, and none of these meanings will ever contradict the other. Instead, they will complement, expand and bring more depth and fuller meaning to that particular scripture.

Paul said in, 1 Corinthians 13:12, "For **now** we **see** in a **mirror**, dimly, but then face to face. **Now** I know in part, but then I shall know just as I also am known."

In my opinion, there is no Christian dead or alive as far as I am aware that can boast that they have 100% revelation and understanding of the whole word of God and His ways, from Genesis to Revelation! Anyone who claims that they do, I might suspect that they are operating in subtle pride. However, I may be wrong about this, but I have not come across, nor heard of, any, and I humbly stand to be corrected if any exist.

So, when it seems, or sound as if we contradict each other in interpretation and doctrines, if we have love one for another, we will pray and take it back to the Lord in prayer. We will not attack or scandalise one another. The Lord says in **John 13:34-35**, "A new commandment I give to you, that you **love one another**; as I have **love**d you, that you also **love one another**. By this all will know that you are My disciples, if you have **love** for **one another**."

The Bible speaks often of the need to love each other. Consider the following scriptures:

John 15:12
"This is my commandment, that you **love one another,** as I have **love**d you."

John 15:17
"These things I command you, that you love one another."

Romans 12:10
"Be kindly affectionate to **one another** with brotherly **love**, in honour giving preference to **one another**."

Galatians 5:13
"For you, brethren, have been called to liberty; only do not use liberty as an opportunity for the flesh, but through **love** serve **one another**."

Ephesians 4:2
"With all lowliness and gentleness, with longsuffering, bearing with **one another** in **love**."

There are a lot of scriptures that tells us this same thing over and over. The Lord says BY THIS - that is, **LOVING ONE ANOTHER - ALL MEN WILL KNOW** THAT WE ARE HIS DISCIPLES.

Why do we find it difficult to convince the world, oftentimes, that we are truly of the Lord? When one of us falls, some of us behave like we have to take vengeance for God, not remembering the teaching of Christ in Jn. 8:7 concerning the woman caught in adultery. "So when they continued asking Him, He raised Himself up and said to them, '*He who is <u>without sin</u> among you*, let him throw a stone at her first'." A little later in that same chapter, in verse 9, the Bible tells us, "Then those who heard *it*, being convicted by *their* conscience, went out one by one, beginning with the oldest *even* to the last."

Sometimes I believe that those who dragged the woman to Christ behaved more honourably than some parts of our churches today. At least they were honest by submitting to the conviction of their conscience.

The Lord has allowed me observe a few different denominations, groups and cultures, and I have noticed that our culture and backgrounds do indeed influence our conduct in the house of God, so much so that, except those who are really desiring to truly grow and submit totally to the word, our culture and background tend to overshadow what we know to be the truth. There can be a very thin line, if allowed, between respect and worship not to God, but to man, in His house amongst His children. This can so easily, in very subtle ways, create doorways for the enemy to start to infiltrate ministries. The enemy will not be afraid of you because you go to church or even make your abode there. He is afraid of you if you understand who you are in Christ, know the word, and are *submitted* to it in total obedience!

Everything in life revolves around sowing and reaping. It is a fundamental spiritual law, and you believing in it or not does not affect the law in any way whatsoever. When we are submitted to the Lord, His Spirit and His word, the enemy has no choice but to submit to us. In other words, when we sow submission to the Lord and His word, we reap submission from demons and circumstances of life! The Lord has shown me the manifestation of this in the spirit realm, and I know it's the best, and most glorious, way for a Christian to live and walk. Our level of submission to God and His word will determine our level of authority over ungodly entities and situations. We already have the authority in Christ that He gave to us; however, we don't all manifest it. How do you command what you submit yourself to? When we are not submitted to God and His word, but will rather submit to the dictates of our flesh and the things of the enemy, we cannot, by the same token, expect to take authority over demons and succeed.

This life that we live does not belong to us! God sat down, looked into the future of mankind, and decided He would need a child for such a time as this to establish His will on earth. He created the life, knowing the end from the beginning, and sent you to live it out. If He did not create your life and send you out here, you would not even be in existence! So the life that you live, believing that you can do what you like with it, is not yours. It belongs to God!

If it were yours, you would be able to hold death back when it comes. Ninety-five percent of the time, we don't even know when death is coming! There is so much we do not even know, but because God has given us a free will, which He will never violate, we let the enemy deceive us into thinking that we have the right to do as we please with the life that God has given us. If that were true, we should then be able to hold death back when it comes and dictate where we spend eternity! Once out of our earthly vessels that have been given to us to function here on earth, we have absolutely no control over where our soul spends eternity, except if we have given that life back to God through Christ Jesus while here and lived it out according to His law, which is His word, according to the holy Bible.

Ecclesiastes 8:8
"No one has **power** over the spirit to retain the spirit, and no one has **power** in the day of death. There is no release from that war, and wickedness will not deliver those who are **give**n to **it**."

Even when we get to heaven, we will continue to learn about God, as far as I am concerned, as I know God is infinite.

He is the source and infinity of life, time, space, power, creation and even eternity. In other words, life, time, space, power, creation, and even eternity exist in Him! Simply put, He is the limitless one of the entire universe. He is the source and infinity of all power in the universe and beyond! This is who I have come to understand Him to be.

This same God has adopted you and me into sonship through redemption, the gift of eternal life, and has declared over and over in His word, "FEAR NOT"! So, of whom should you be afraid? And who ought you to fear, but God? We ought to fear God and His laws, and not man or the Devil.

The enemy and his agents control men through deception, lies and fear, but the Lord Jesus declared, "You shall **know the truth** and **the truth shall make you free**"! The only way to get out from under the control of deception, lies and fear, is to seek, know and believe in the truth of the word of God and ensure to live in, and by, it! To date, the enemy still attacks people through fear, despite the passage of scripture that says, in Isaiah14:15-17:

Yet you [the devil] shall be brought down to Sheol, to the lowest depths of the Pit. Those who see you will **gaze at you,** [as in disbelief] *and* consider you, *saying:* "Is this the man who made the earth tremble, who shook kingdoms, who made the world as a wilderness and destroyed its cities, who did not open the house of his prisoners?"

We need not be afraid. We only need to trust our Heavenly Father totally, even when we do not see the manifestations that we expect. We should still trust Him enough to know that He knows what He is doing and what is best for us. Our most important focus should be on God, our Lord Jesus, the Holy Spirit, the word of God and submitting to it and the purpose for which He created and sent us here. All our energy, plans and pursuit in life should be geared towards fulfilling that purpose and calling. Every other fleshly pursuit is nothing but vanity, if it is not for God's glory, those things will not count when we stand before Him to give an account of the life that He has given to us to use.

Those who are truly watching and praying understand that the night is far spent, and dawn has come. This is the time to rise out of our ruts, dust ourselves up, and begin to stir our spirits up in prayer, abiding in the word and seeking the Lord like never before!

For those who are already blazing that trail, I give God glory.

It is never too late to return to the Lord with a truly repentant heart, except when we are already physically dead. The Lord is ever so glad when a lost or backsliding child returns home. We always have the cross and the blood before us for a perpetual place to return, lay it all down, and cleanse ourselves by the shed blood of Christ whenever needed. It is our open doorway to the throne room of the Father, whose arms are forever opened to welcome His children because of His covenant and unfailing love for us.

The Bible declares that nothing shall separate us from God's love. "For I am persuaded that neither death nor life, nor angels nor principalities nor powers, nor things present nor things to come, nor height nor depth, nor any other created thing, shall

Abiding In Love

be able to separate us from the love of God which is in Christ Jesus our Lord" (Romans 8:38-39).

God's love is unfailing, and He desires the very best for us always. Even when we do not fully understand His ways, but resolve in our hearts to trust Him, come what may, He will always come through for us. I know this because my life is a living testimony. I have seen too much of God's faithfulness, even in the most unlikely situations. I call him the "bestest" Dad in the entire universe and beyond - the very best any child could ever wish for! My son, at four years old, calls me the "bestest mum in the whole world!"

Very hard days are coming to test those that live on the face of the earth. We have no answers for what is coming, except in Christ. This is the time for every serious-minded Christian to re-examine their spiritual lives and their walk with God. This is the time to truly and fully understand our true identity as those belonging to Christ. It is the time to bury ourselves back in the word and be like the Berean Christians, to know and understand the word of God for ourselves, and let it take root in our hearts. It is the time to be like the sons of Issachar.

"Then the brethren immediately sent Paul and Silas away by night to Berea. When they arrived, they went into the synagogue of the Jews. These were more fair-minded than those in Thessalonica, in that *they received the word with all readiness, and* **searched the Scriptures daily to find out** *whether these things were so. Therefore many of them believed* and also not a few of the Greeks, prominent women as well as men" (Acts 17:10-12).

It is time for us to be like the sons of Issachar, **who** had **understanding** of the **times** to know what Israel (the Church) ought to do (1 Chronicles 12:32).

Chapter 15

Knowing Who We Are

I was in the top deck of a bus recently when I suddenly felt a terrible sense of grief and anxiety overwhelm me, and I became instantly alert, thinking I was coming under some kind of spiritual attack, as I knew I had nothing to make me feel that way in the natural. I immediately began to pray in the spirit and to take authority over my surrounding atmosphere, bringing it under the blood covering. Then I heard the Lord say, "You are not being attacked. You are picking up the earth's burden". (I have heard it said that the Lord does not give burdens, he removes it). Every real intercessor knows that is not true when it comes to prayer. It is written in Matthew 11:30

"For My yoke is easy and *My burden* is light." (Bold and italics mine.) The Lord removes the enemy's burden off of us because it is oppressive. However when he needs us to pray his will, he places into our spirit man, a burden or an urgent need or urge to pray and this type of burden is not oppressive – instead, it is compassionate. I know this from experience.

I was surprised to hear that, as I had never heard anything like that before, nor did I know the earth had emotions, and I was not sure what to make of it. He continued and said, "She, the earth, has seen evil in her days, but not such that is about to come upon the face of the earth to test, try and persecute those that are on the earth". Then I remembered the scripture that said, in **Matthew 24:21**, "For then there **will** be great **tribula-**

tion, such as has not been since the beginning of the **world** until this time, no, nor ever shall be."

I began to pray in the spirit, and I am still praying. I am also crying out to God to let the "spirit of prayer" hit and invade the entire body of Christ like thunder and lightning with the force of the tsunami multiplied in seven-million fold, and to let it spread like an uncontrollable wild fire, igniting and setting the body of Christ ablaze, so that there will be such an outcry of prayer from the body of Christ to the throne room of God, such as has never been heard before since the creation of man until now. There will be a shaking in the heavens and on earth, and after that, there will be a re-alignment of things in the heavens and on earth, even as prophecy begins to unfold and the will of God becomes established on earth, as it is in heaven! We are the light of the world and the salt of the earth and, as Christ's body on earth, most parts simply have not come to a full realisation; i.e., they have not been grounded in the revelation and understanding of our true identity in Christ here on earth. We have allowed, and accepted, the enemy's **intimidation, lies, deception** and **fear** to infiltrate our lives and the body, despite the fact that we have the truth of God's word. We live according to the image we have of ourselves instead of living in and through the image of Christ. We can do this by living according to the word.

We are Heaven's Ambassadors on earth, and an Ambassador in the natural has to fully understand the nature, the culture and politics of the place he's been sent to and how they operate. Also, he will be there to totally and fully represent his home country in a very determined and focused attitude and will do nothing to neither bring shame to his kingdom nor compromise the policies of his Country. When the Bible says, "my people perish for lack of knowledge", I believe it is not just knowledge of the word only, but also of the world that we live in. Lack of knowledge can keep you in ignorance of the true state of things. However, when we are in deep fellowship with the Holy Spirit, He will tell us things to come, even hidden things that you would normally not have been able to know on your own. So we as citizens of the heavenly glory, ought to manifest ourselves as Heavens Ambassadors that we are.

Intimidation. The very last thing the enemy wants is for us as Christians to understand our true identity and walk in it because he knows that, when that begins to happen, he is in more trouble. However, read God's words below.

Proverbs 28:1
"The wicked flee when no one pursues, *but the righteous are bold as a lion.*"

Acts 4:13
"Now when they saw the **boldness** of Peter and John, and perceived that they were uneducated and untrained men, they *marvelled*; and they *realized* that they had been with Jesus."

It was the *boldness* that they saw in Peter and John that caused them to marvel (something that causes wonder, admiration, or astonishment) and brought them to the realization (to grasp or understand clearly) that these men were of Christ! A lot of Christians are becoming less bold at declaring the truth of the word of God, even from the pulpits because they want to be more "user friendly" and are afraid of persecutions, forgetting the words of Jesus that declares.

John 16:33
"These things I have spoken to you, that in me you may have peace. In the **world** you **will** have **tribulation**; but be of good cheer, **I have** *overcome* **the world.**"

And we are in him!
Matthew 10:16
"Behold, I send you out as sheep in the midst of wolves. *Therefore be wise as serpents and harmless as doves.*"

This is one of the most powerful scriptures for the days that are ahead, but we will not be able to manifest this if we are not grounded in the word, in the Spirit and in knowing who we are!

Mark 4:16-17
These likewise are the ones sown on stony ground who, when they hear the word, immediately receive it with gladness; and they *have no root in themselves* [in other words, they did not take the time to get grounded in the word] and so endure only for a time. Afterward, when tribulation or ***persecution arises for the word's sake***, immediately they stumble.

We should truly examine ourselves and consider what type of ground we are, in relation to God's word, because persecutory laws are beginning to rear their heads all over the place under the guise of political correctness, and one of their main purposes is to intimidate and persecute the real children of God from crying out against unrighteousness according to the word of God in the lands, forgetting that the earth is the Lord's and its fullness thereof! I say the real children of God because a real child of God will uphold and honour the words and laws of God. Heaven is His throne, and the earth is His footstool. The word of God will be fulfilled; for the very earth where all these are happening was created by that same word of God and is still being upheld by the word of God; therefore, it will be judged by the word of God, whether the wheat and the tares believe it or not!

Servants of God are being monitored for what they say out of the pulpits, and some of them already feel intimidated for fear of persecution. The exact same thing was done to Christ in the book of **Luke (20:20)**. *"So they watched Him, and sent spies who pretended to be righteous, that they might seize on His words, in order to deliver Him to the power and the authority of the governor." (underline mine).*

However, the Lords tells us in his word not to fear. As **Matthew 10:28** tells us, "And do **not** fear **those who kill** the **body** but cannot **kill** the **soul**. But rather fear Him **who** is able to destroy both **soul** and **body** in hell." Whether we die out of persecution or naturally, the Lord is in control of our lives, and He has declared that He will not leave us, nor forsake us!

Consider Hebrew 13:5-6:

"*Let your* conduct *be* without covetousness; *be* content with such things as you have. For He Himself has said, '*I will never leave you nor forsake you*'" So we may boldly say: '*The LORD is my helper; I will not fear. What can man do to me?*'

A message came forth recently during a prayer meeting declaring that the angels that gather are already at work, gathering the tares from the wheat, and even the wheat that has become corrupted on the inside but still looks like wheat on the outside will be gathered away from the midst of the good wheat!

We are in the world, but not of it. We have come out of eternity (God's realm) into time for a purpose and will return there when we are done on earth! Hence, the Bible declares, in Ecclesiastes 3:11, **"He has made everything beautiful in its time. Also *He (The Lord) has put eternity in their (men's) hearts*,** except that no one can find out the work that God does from beginning to end."

We may not be able to find out on this side of life, but we can trust that, since He created our lives and we are willing to surrender them back to Him in faith and trust, then is He able to lead, guide and establish our destiny according to the purpose for which He created us in the first place.

Our entire lifetime here on earth is like a single drop of water in an ocean. So what manner of people are we if we allow our lives to be so wrapped up in worldly affairs and pay little attention to what we sow into the spirit realm when we cannot take a pin with us out of the world when we die, but will meet in eternity, for all eternity, those things we have sown in the spirit!

The Lord tells us, "Do not lay up for yourselves treasures on earth, where moth and rust destroy and where thieves break in and steal; but lay up for yourselves treasures in Heaven, where neither moth nor rust destroys and where thieves do not break in and steal. For *where your treasure is, there your heart will be also.*"

Until our hearts are totally surrendered to the Lord in spirit and in truth, we will not achieve much spiritually. If our treasures are being laid up in Heaven, then our hearts will also be there and will manifest from that realm of glory. As 1 John 2:15 says, "Do not love the world or the things in the world. If anyone loves the world, the love of the Father is not in him." As a man thinks in his heart so is he (Prov 23:7).

Solomon, a man of great wisdom finally concludes about life:

Ecclesiastes 12:13
"Let us hear the conclusion of the whole matter: **<u>Fear God and keep His commandment,</u> for this is man's all.**" (Underline and bold mine)

I pray daily for the manifestation of the godly wisdom already resident within me in the person of the Holy Spirit, but I will not put my confidence in it until I know, without an iota of a doubt that my heart, mind, soul and will are one hundred percent surrendered unreservedly to the Lord! Solomon was given so much wisdom, yet his heart turned away from his God!

1 Kings 4:29
"And God gave **Solomon** wisdom and exceedingly great understanding, and largeness of **heart** like the sand on the seashore."

However:

> But King Solomon *loved* (a heart affair) many foreign women, as well as the daughter of Pharaoh: women of the Moabites, Ammonites, Edomites, Sidonians, *and* Hittites— from the nations of whom the LORD had said to the children of Israel, "You shall not intermarry with them, nor they with you. Surely they will turn away your hearts after their gods." Solomon **clung** to these in love. And he had seven hundred wives, princesses, and three hundred concubines; *and his wives turned away his heart.* For it was so, when Solomon was old, that *his wives turned his heart after other gods; and his heart was not loyal to the LORD his God, as was the heart of his father David.* For *Solomon went after Ashtoreth the*

goddess of the Sidonians, and after Milcom the abomination of the Ammonites. Solomon did evil in the sight of the LORD, and did not fully follow the LORD, as did his father David. <u>Then Solomon built a high place for Chemosh the abomination of Moab, on the hill that is east of Jerusalem, and for Molech the abomination of the people of Ammon. And he did likewise for all his foreign wives, who burned incense and sacrificed to their gods.</u> So the LORD became angry with Solomon, because *his heart had turned from the LORD God of Israel, who had appeared to him twice, and had commanded him concerning this thing, that he should not go after other gods; but he did not keep what the LORD had commanded.* Therefore the LORD said to Solomon, "Because you have done this, and have not kept my covenant and my statutes, which I have commanded you, I will surely tear the kingdom away from you and give it to your servant. Nevertheless I will not do it in your days, for the sake of your father David; I will tear it out of the hand of your son. However I will not tear away the whole kingdom; I will give one tribe to your son for the sake of my servant David, and for the sake of Jerusalem which I have chosen."

It is very sad indeed that a man who received so much blessings and so much godly wisdom from the one true source ended up like this.

I have read many testimonies of Christians visiting heaven and meeting with saints who have already passed on, even King David. I have heard a lot of names, but never Solomon's. I wonder where he is, and why no one visiting heaven has yet met him.

Eternal separation from God is what men ought to dread most in life, for they originated from Him and should return to Him. I strongly suspect that that the burning flames of hell are nothing compared to the soul torture and agony of eternal separation from God.

Chapter 16

Staying Strong and Focused

Mark 10:29-31
So Jesus answered and said, "Assuredly, I say to you, there is no one who has left house or brothers or sisters or father or mother or wife or children or lands, for My sake and the gospel's, who shall not receive a hundredfold now in this time—houses and brothers and sisters and mothers and children and lands, *with persecutions*—and in the age to come, eternal life. But many *who are* first will be last, and the last first."

A lot of us like to claim this passage, except for the *persecutions*, but they are part of the package! If they persecuted Christ, why should we expect any less? But the good news is that now we have the VICTORY in Christ Jesus!

Also, it is written in the book of Daniel that those who know their God shall do exploits!

How much do you really and honestly know your God? Do you truly and honestly know Him, His word, His will, and His ways? Or do you just assume that you do based on you being born again and your service in the house of God?

Even if you mentally know every verse of the Bible from Genesis to Revelation, how much have you meditated on them to receive true revelation and understanding? We have to bring ourselves to the place of such intimacy with our Heavenly Father and our Precious Lord and Saviour Jesus Christ through His word and His Holy Spirit, so much so that we become extraordinarily sensitive, even to his slightest stir! We will know to stand when He is standing, sit when He is sitting, move when He is moving, and speak when He is speaking! We will look and see as He does, listen and hear as He does, and endeavour to love as He loves until His "heartbeat" becomes ours, and we become His true image here on earth and manifest our heavenly kingdom daily in this earthly realm!

This may seem, to some, to be an impossible task to achieve. It is my desperate desire, and I believe without any shadow of doubt that it is achievable because the word of God already declares us so, if we are of, and in, Christ! And, because the word of God already declares us so, I desire its materialization and physical manifestations in my life, and I know it will come only through walking in total and uncompromising obedience to His word and His will - through a life of absolute surrender to Him!

We have His name. "At the name of Jesus, every knee shall bow!" We have His blood and His word. The Bible declares that "and they overcame him - the devil by the blood of the lamb and the words of their testimony". We have his Spirit! The Bible declares that "greater is He that is in us that is, the Holy Spirit of God, than he that is in the world."

Acts 4:23-31

And being let go, they went to their own *companions* and reported all that the chief priests and elders had said to them. So when they heard that, they raised their voice to God with one accord and said: "Lord, You *are* God, who made heaven and earth and the sea, and all that is in them, who by the mouth of your servant David have said:

> *'Why did the nations rage, and the people plot vain things? The kings of the earth took their stand, and the rulers were gathered together against the LORD and against His Christ.'*

"For truly against Your holy Servant Jesus, whom You anointed, both Herod and Pontius Pilate, with the

Gentiles and the people of Israel, were gathered together to do whatever Your hand and Your purpose determined before to be done. Now, Lord, look on their threats, and **grant to your servants that with all boldness they may speak your word, by stretching out your hand to heal, and that signs and wonders may be done through the name of your holy Servant Jesus."**

And when they had prayed, the place where they were assembled together was shaken; and they were all filled with the Holy Spirit, and they spoke the word of God with *boldness.*

This is what ought to be happening amongst all Christians now!

Philippians 1:19-21
"For I know that this will turn out for my deliverance through your prayer and the supply of the Spirit of Jesus Christ, according to my earnest expectation and hope that in nothing I shall be ashamed, **but with all boldness**, as always, so now also Christ will be magnified in my body, whether by life or by death. For to me, to live *is* Christ, and to die *is* gain."

Sadly, many Christians do not choose to live in boldness. Instead, they fall prey to the lies and intimidation of Satan. There are many passages in the Bible that warn against choosing to follow the lies of devil rather than believing the truth of God's word.

John 8:44
"You are of your father the devil and the desires of your father you want to do. He was a murderer from the beginning, and *does not stand in the truth, because there is no truth in him. When he speaks a lie, he speaks from his own resources, for he is a liar and the father of it"*.

Revelation 12:9
"So **the great dragon** was cast out, that serpent of old, called **the** Devil and Satan, *__who deceives the whole world;__* he was cast to **the** earth, and his angels were cast out with him."

Luke 21:8
"And He said: *'Take heed that you **not be deceived**. For many will come in my name, saying, "I am He," and, "The time has drawn near." Therefore do **not** go after them'."

1 Corinthians 6:9
"Do you **not** know that the unrighteous will **not** inherit the kingdom of God? Do **not** be **deceived**. Neither fornicators, nor idolaters, nor adulterers, nor homosexuals, nor sodomites..."

1 Corinthians 15:33
"Do **not** be **deceived**: 'Evil Company corrupts good habits.'

Galatians 6:7
"Do **not** be **deceived**; God is **not** mocked; for whatever a man sows, that he will also reap."

Seeing these words, we need to carefully contemplate what we ought to do. The Lord said, "If you love me, obey my commandments." Several verses in the Bible encourage us to do just that.

1 John 5:3
"For this **is** the love of God, that we keep His **commandment**s. And His **commandment**s are **not burdensome**."

1 John 2:28
"And now, little children, abide in Him, that when He appears, we may have confidence and not be **ashamed** before Him at **His coming**."

Matthew 25: 7-8
"Then all those virgins arose and trimmed their lamps. And the foolish said to the wise, 'Give us some of your oil, <u>for our lamps are going out</u>'."

As the Church is being stirred up, so we also need to be trimming our lamps - reviving ourselves, that is, and ensuring we have enough oil - the true knowledge of God's word to carry us through so that we do not have to start asking for knowledge and understanding of the word when we need to already have known and understood what we ought to do and when.

Things are going to start happening very quickly, and we should be ready to teach and assist those who are escaping the world and running into the kingdom of God. We should not start paying undue attention to ourselves and those of us who have been in the kingdom a long time but could not be bothered to acquire reasonable amounts of extra oil in our vessels because we gave it no priority.

The very days are being shortened, and the Bible says that even the very elect will be deceived except the days are shortened. I see a lot of confusion already, and the falling away has begun in preparation for the persecution of the true church. Even old Christians are beginning to ask for explanations of what is going on, as they lack true revelation and understanding of what they see. They are already requesting some of the others' oil, as their knowledge of the word is not sufficient to carry them through. The sad thing to see is that so many Christians are undiscerning of things that are happening behind the current events of things.

The Bible says, "my people are destroyed – made poor, become hard pressed, subjected to oppression for lack of knowledge." This is not just of the word of God, but also of the world that we live in. We will be very amazed when we genuinely begin to abide in the word of God and let it abide in us. When we genuinely abide in the Holy Spirit of the living God, have our MIND stayed on the word and on the Lord, and abide in the place of "praying always", the Lord will begin to open our eyes and heart of understanding, as He does not desire that we remain in ignorance. **The level of your hunger will determine the level of your infilling, revelation and understanding.** I have heard Christians sing and pray that the Lord come and quench the thirsting of our souls. I don't ever sing or pray that. I ask for a FILLING instead. I don't ever want my hunger and thirst for Him to be quenched. I ask for an unquenchable hunger and thirst instead.

David said in Psalm 42:1 As the deer pants for the water brooks, So pants my soul for You, O God.

The confusion and deception that have started to go forth will cause many to stumble, except they are thoroughly rooted and grounded in the word. The reason for that is that most of us are still so earthly bound when we should be soaring up high and above, like the Eagle and seeing way above and beyond the current events. We ought to be riding on the current of the winds of the movement of the Spirit of the living God! When we are able to do that, we will not be confused because we will see with clarity, understand situations, and know what we ought to do, like the sons of Issachar.

For whatever time we have left, we need to bury our attention in the word, acquiring as much extra oil as we can for those of us who have not yet made it our utmost priority to do so, to see us through and revive our altars of prayer in total reverential fear of and submission to God. Obedience to His word and submission to His will! We need to have our focus fixed on him, as the Eagle fixes its focus upon the sun in times of adversity.

Chapter 17

Those Who Sell

Matthew 25:9-10
"But the wise answered, saying, 'No, lest there should not be enough for us and you; but go rather to those who sell, and buy for yourselves.' And while they went to buy, the bridegroom came, and those who were ready went in with him to the wedding; and the door was shut."

The important question in these verses is: *Who are those who sell?* For quite some time, I have always thought those who sell were the Bible teachers, pastors, ministers, and the like until the Holy Spirit asked me, "How can they be, when they themselves are part of the wise or foolish virgins?"

I was surprised and started to pray for understanding. I am aware that the literal interpretation of this is lack of preparedness by the foolish virgins. However, the Holy Spirit finally took me to the book of Isaiah, chapter 11.

> There shall come forth a Rod from the stem of Jesse, and a Branch shall grow out of his roots. The Spirit of the LORD shall rest upon Him, The Spirit of wisdom and understanding, The Spirit of counsel and might, The Spirit of knowledge and of the fear of the LORD.

These are the seven Spirits of God. As I prayerfully meditated upon this passage of scripture, the Holy Spirit brought me to the understanding of it. Everything that Christ was, and is, He died for us to have and become. We come to this revelation and understanding through the knowledge of the word. We have to study it, believe it, agree with it, and submit to it in total trust and obedience.

Hebrew 3:12-15 says, "*Beware, brethren, lest there be in any of you **an evil heart of unbelief** in departing from the living God; but exhort one another daily, while it is called 'Today,' lest any of you be hardened through the deceitfulness of sin. **For we have become partakers of Christ** if we hold the beginning of our confidence steadfast to the end, while it is said: 'Today, if you will hear His voice, do not harden your hearts as in the rebellion'.*"

The Bible says, in Colossians 2:10 that we are complete in Christ.

2 Peter 1:4 says we are partakers of His divine nature.
Hebrews 3:14 says we are made perfect in Christ.
Romans 8:17 says we are joint heirs with Christ.
Colossians 1:12 says we are partakers of the inheritance.
John 4:17 Love has been perfected among us in this: that we may have boldness in the Day of Judgment; **because as He is, so are we in this world.**

In the book of Revelation 5:6, it says, "And I looked, and behold, in the midst of the throne and of the four living creatures, and in the midst of the elders, stood a Lamb as though it had been slain, having seven horns and seven eyes, which are **the seven Spirits of God sent out into all the earth.**"

This clearly indicates that the seven Spirits of God are on earth with us.

Seven is God's perfect number, indicating the complete fullness of the Holy Spirit. The Bible tells us that Christ had the Holy Spirit without measure, confirming Isaiah 11:2. These seven Spirits of God have their own distinct manifestations, as clearly outlined in Isaiah 11:2, all complete in the person of the Holy Spirit.

Eph 5:18 tells us to be filled with the Spirit. If it were not possible to become filled, we would not have been commanded to. The Bible also says, in 1 John 4:17, that as the Lord is, so are we in this world!

In 2 Corinthians 5:17, the Bible tells us we are new creations.

1 Corinthians 6:19 say we are the temple of the Holy Spirit.

Ephesians 1:13 says we are sealed with the Holy Spirit of promise.

Since Christ has the Spirit without measure, it goes to show that we ought to stay filled with the Spirit continuously. Much as this scripture is true, the reality or manifestation of it however, now depends on our receiving this truth, accepting it, believing it, and totally submitting to it for these truths to fully manifest in our lives.

The Spirit of the Lord is the Spirit of Dominion that gives you boldness from an understanding of your true identity in Christ and produces in you, supernatural confidence that will cause you to confront and take charge of whatever situation or challenges you may face, knowing whose child you are, and that the greater one lives in you.

It was the Spirit that came upon David as an untrained youth when he chose to go and face Goliath, whilst King Saul and all his mighty army cowered in fear of Goliath. It caused David to dominate the challenge and brought forth victory for Israel. It was also the Spirit that came upon him, along with the Spirit of Might when he slew the Lion and the Bear that tried to kill a lamb out of his father's flock (1 Samuel 17).

The Spirit of Wisdom will give you depth of insight into what your natural mind could never comprehend. It will cause you to see and understand what others do not see, and it will always give you an edge over others and over all situations. It brings you an inner understanding and confidence that propels you to take the right action in any given situation.

Proverbs 4:7 declares, "Wisdom *is* the principal thing; *Therefore* get wisdom. And in all your getting, get understanding."

Later in Proverbs (8:12), we read, "I, wisdom, dwell with prudence, and find out knowledge *and* discretion."

Psalm 111:10
"**The fear of the LORD is the** beginning **of** wisdom; A good understanding have all those who do His commandments. His praise endures forever."

Proverbs 9:10
"The **fear of the LORD is the** beginning **of** wisdom, and **the** knowledge **of the** Holy One is understanding."

The Spirit of Understanding goes hand in hand with the Spirit of Revelation and of wisdom, like the threefold cord that cannot be easily broken or separated. Revelation will always bring you understanding, and understanding will produce the wisdom to act wisely.

The Bible says, in 1 Cor. 2:16, that we have the mind of Christ. Along this same vein, Matthew 13:11 says, "He answered and said to them, 'Because *it has been given to you* to know the mysteries of the kingdom of heaven, but to them it has not been given...'."

This was when the disciples asked Christ why He spoke to the people in parables. This clearly shows that we have the power, and ability, to understand if we will meditate on the word and seek understanding of it.

The Spirit of Counsel guides and leads you in the way you should go. It directs you in a situation that you would normally not know how to handle or not know what to do when you are in the middle of it. He leads, and directs, you, even when it makes absolutely no sense to your natural mind. As a result, your inner peace is restored.

Psalm 23:2-3 says, "He makes me to lie down in green pastures; He *leads* me beside the still waters. He restores my soul. He *leads* me in the paths of righteousness for His name's sake."

Psalm 16:7
"I will bless the LORD, who *has given me counsel;* My heart also instructs me in the **night season**s."

Proverbs 19:20
"Listen to **counsel** and receive instruction, that you may be wise in your latter days."

Proverbs 24:6
"For by wise **counsel** you will wage your own war, and in a multitude of **counsel**lors there is safety."

Isaiah 30:21
"Your ears shall hear a word behind you, saying, 'This *is* the way, walk in it,' whenever you turn to the right hand, or whenever you turn to the left."

In the days that are ahead, we are going to need these manifestations of the Holy Spirit like never before because there will be a lot of confusion for people who will not be sure of what to do or where to go.

Once, I was desperately in need of something and had no clue how to get it. I began to fast and pray. After a few days of fasting and praying, I suddenly felt the strong urge to go to a particular office that I had no business going to as of that time. I reluctantly obeyed, and I went. I got there, stood around, and asked myself why I had come and what I was doing there. Almost immediately, I felt the urge to pray some more, so I looked for a quiet corner and began to pray.

As I was praying, I heard, "go and meet so and so." I was given a name I had never heard of before. I paused, thought about it a while, and stepped out of the corner into the open, where I saw a lady walking by. I stopped her and asked if she worked there, and she answered yes. I then asked her if she knew anyone by the name the Lord had given me, and she said yes, and that the person whose name I had asked for is the assistant director for a particular department!

Great surprise and excitement came over me as I began to follow her direction to the office. When I walked into the reception area, I was not sure what to say, so I asked for a pen and paper and scribbled a small note to the person, explaining that I was led to come see them, and I hoped they won't ask me, "By whom?" If they had, then I would have no choice, but to tell them 'by God'.

The note was taken in, and I was shortly summoned. I was asked how I could be helped, and I explained what I wanted. I was turned down. Just as I turned around to leave the office thanking the Lord quietly, but feeling confused, knowing I had never met this person, nor known their name before, I was asked to stop just before opening the office door to walk out and was told to come back the following Tuesday! The end of the story was, I got exactly what I wanted!

That was the Spirit of Counsel at work, as there is no way I could ever have chosen to go there on my own when I did. Also, there is no way I could have known that person's name! It would never have crossed my mind, in a hundred years, to go to them, since I never even knew them, or met them before.

We are going to need a lot of such manifestations in the days that are ahead because the confusion and anxiety will not be receding. It will be like the prophecy over Zion in the book of Isaiah, chapter 60, verses 1-3.

The Spirit of Might will cause you to do extraordinary things and accomplish feats that you could never achieve in your own natural might. The Spirit of might was in Samson (Judges 14:5-6). "So Samson went down to Timnah with his father and mother, and came to the vineyards of Timnah. Now *to his* surprise, a young lion *came* roaring against him. And the Spirit of the LORD came mightily upon him, and he tore the lion apart as one would have torn apart a young goat, though *he had* nothing in his hand. But he did not tell his father or his mother what he had done."

Later on in the book of Judges (15:14-15), the story of Samson continues. "When he came to Lehi, the Philistines came shouting against him. Then the Spirit of the LORD came mightily upon him; and the ropes that *were* on his arms became like flax that is burned with fire, and his bonds broke loose from his hands. He found a fresh jawbone of a donkey, reached out his hand and took it, and killed a thousand men with it."

David also manifested this same Spirit in his account before King Saul of his encounter with the Bear and a Lion in 1 Samuel 17.

When he comes on you, he overrides your physical ability and senses and empowers you to do that which is usually impossible. He takes total control until he is done.

Paul prayed that the believer would have, and manifest it, in Ephesians 3:14-16. "For this reason I bow my knees to the Father of our Lord Jesus Christ, from whom the whole family in heaven and earth is named, that He would grant you, according to the riches of His glory, to be strengthened with might through his Spirit in the inner man...."

The Spirit of Knowledge

The Spirit of Knowledge deposits in you acute, precise and unshakable knowledge about things, people and situations. It is supernatural knowledge that surpasses natural knowledge. You just know that you know, irrespective of any confronting contradictions. It is totally different from head knowledge. It is a confident, rigid knowledge in your spirit that sometimes contradicts your head knowledge. Once you come to recognise it, you just learn to follow it, irrespective of any contradictory outer circumstance.

It puts you ahead of a situation and gives you peace. The Lord says his people perish for lack of it.

1 Corinthians 2:9-12 *says, "Eye has not seen, nor ear heard, nor have entered into the heart of man the things which God has prepared for those who love Him."* But God has revealed *them* to us through His Spirit. For the Spirit searches all things, yes, the deep things of God. For what man knows the things of a man except the spirit of the man which is in him? Even so no one knows the things of God except the Spirit of God.

Now we have received, not the spirit of the world, but the Spirit who is from God, that we might *know* the things that have been freely given to us by God."

Eph.3:17-19 further explains it. "...that Christ may dwell in your hearts through faith; that you, being rooted and grounded in love, may be able to comprehend with all the saints what *is* the width and length and depth and height—to *know* (spiritual knowledge) the love of Christ *which passes knowledge (natural knowledge);* that you may be filled with all the fullness of God."

Once I had gone with a friend to a Christian conference and, as we were walking back to the car, I spun round and pointed at her, telling her she was going to be pregnant and have a baby boy! We were not even talking about anything personal, and there was no natural reason for me to have said that because she had since been separated from her husband who was already living with another woman! She got upset and told me to stop it, if it was some kind of a joke. She was very angry at the man and wanted nothing to do with him, let alone have more children with him, but I just knew supernaturally without an iota of doubt that she was going to have another boy with this same man!

Two years later, she delivered a baby boy for him. After that she came to me and said she wanted to cut her tubes to prevent having another child. We were standing in my kitchen. I looked at her and told her that, even if she did, the tubes would unwind, come back together, and she would still have another child! I told her there is one more baby to come. She looked at me with a kind of a weird and shocked expression, but this time she did not argue. Two years and three months later, she had a baby girl, and she was done.

The circumstance surrounding her that I knew was contradictory to what I was saying. However, I just knew that I knew on the inside. I have experienced that a lot of times, even with people I have never met. Sometimes all I need is to hear their names, and the Spirit of knowledge takes over. Sometimes even the names of people I have never met, I just know. That is the working of the Spirit of Knowledge, and it has nothing to do with me, but it is entirely of the Holy Spirit, as He chooses to manifest it when He wills.

The Spirit of the Fear of the Lord. This is the Spirit of reverence that causes you to exalt God above all else, and the Bible tells us that the "fear of the Lord is the beginning of wisdom".

Those Who Sell

This Spirit brings a reverential fear of God that causes you to rein in all self or fleshly excesses.

It was manifested at the foot of Mt. Sinai. "Now all the people witnessed the thunderings, the lightning flashes, the sound of the trumpet, and the mountain smoking; and when the people saw *it,* they trembled and stood afar off. Then they said to Moses, 'You speak with us, and we will hear; but let not God speak with us, lest we die.' And Moses said to the people, 'Do not fear; for God has come to test you, and that His fear may be before you, so that you may not sin.' So the people stood afar off, but Moses drew near the thick darkness where God *was.*"

Also, in the book of Acts, chapter 5, we read of Ananias and Sapphira:

> But a certain man named Ananias, with Sapphira his wife, sold a possession. And he kept back *part* of the proceeds, his wife also being aware *of it,* and brought a certain part and laid *it* at the apostles' feet. But Peter said, "Ananias, why has Satan filled your heart to lie to the Holy Spirit and keep back *part* of the price of the land for yourself? While it remained, was it not your own? And after it was sold, was it not in your own control? Why have you conceived this thing in your heart? You have not lied to men but to God."
> Then Ananias, hearing these words, fell down and breathed his last. ***So great fear came upon all those who heard these things.*** And the young men arose and wrapped him up, carried *him* out, and buried *him*. (Bold and italics mine)
> Now it was about three hours later when his wife came in, not knowing what had happened. And Peter answered her, "Tell me whether you sold the land for so much?" She said, "Yes, for so much."
> Then Peter said to her, "How is it that you have agreed together to test the Spirit of the Lord? Look, the feet of those who have buried your husband *are* at the door, and they will carry you out." Then immediately she fell down at his feet and breathed her last. And the young

men came in and found her dead, and carrying *her* out, buried *her* by her husband. ***So great fear came upon all the church and upon all who heard these things*** (Acts 5:1-11). (Bold and italics mine)

This spirit also manifested with the Old Testament Prophets.
These are the seven Spirits of God that have been sent forth into all the earth, according to Revelation 5:6. They are those that sell. Paul tells us to be filled with the Spirit, as Christ has the Spirit without measure, and at His coming, we are supposed to truly resemble him spiritually!

1 John 3:2 tells us, "Beloved, now we are children of God; and it has not yet been revealed what we shall be, but we know that when He is revealed, we shall be like Him, for we shall see Him as He is."

It's one thing to have been giving a spiritual garment of righteousness. It's another thing altogether to keep that garment clean in righteousness. I am aware that we are the righteousness of God in Christ, but that is now no excuse to continue to live according to the dictates of our flesh, just because we are His righteousness. We are to work out our individual salvation with fear and trembling, abiding in the word and letting the word abide in us, humbling ourselves in the hands of God and submitting to His word and will for our lives. God is not mocked. Whatever we sow, we shall also reap.

Galatians 6:8
"For he who sows to his flesh will of the flesh **reap corruption**, but he who sows to the Spirit will of the Spirit **reap** everlasting life."

I believe it's never too late for anyone willing to turn their life around now so that our Christian walk will not be in vain. We can always return to the place of the cross for repentance and back to the covenant - the covenant walk with the Lord - the life and walk of obedience.

When we buy from these Seven Spirits that are the seven manifestations of the Holy Spirit, we buy with our hunger and thirst in seeking after Him. The Bible says those that hunger and thirst after righteousness shall be filled (Matt 5:6)! We buy with our time in communion. We buy with our will, by surrendering our will completely and totally to Him. That is when we begin to get transformed into His image in fullness.

For the days that are coming, we need to be closer to the Lord than ever before, grounded in His word more than ever before, and yielded and surrendered to his Spirit like never before.

FINALLY

*I*f you have read this book, it is not by accident. It is the Lord's will that you do. Prayerfully seek Him to let you know what you have been assigned to do in, and for, the body of Christ, or the world, for such a time as this.

It does not matter what you have been through in life, there is a purpose for which you were created and sent here. It is not too late to find it, live it and use it for His glory.

If you are not born again, please pray this prayer with belief in your heart:

> Heavenly Father, I thank you for your great and unfailing love for me - for your patient and longsuffering. I thank you for sending the Lord Jesus to lay His life down for me that I will be reconciled back to You.
>
> Lord Jesus, I thank you for dying for me. I confess and repent of all my sins before you. Cleanse me with your Blood and from all unrighteousness.
>
> I surrender my life to you and ask you to become the Lord of my life. Give me your Holy Spirit, and help me fulfil my new life in you.
>
> Thank you, Lord, for answered prayer. Amen.

After you say this prayer, simply believe in your heart that God has heard and answered you and that all of Heaven is rejoicing that a child of God has returned home to the Father's heart. Look for a GOOD BIBLE. The NEW KING JAMES IN THE AMPLIFIED VERSION is quite good for modern English, or for a more straightforward and modern English version, I like the **World Bible Translation**, easy-to-read version.

Also try reading *Revealing Heaven, Volumes 1& 2* by KAT KERR and *Heaven Awaits the Bride* by ANNA ROUNTREE.

You can also read *The Final Quest* by RICK JOYNER, or *I Believe in Visions* by KENNETH HAGIN. His books are all very good for spiritual growth.

There are many more books that will give you a clearer picture of your heavenly home, your Heavenly Father, your Lord, and the Holy Spirit. If you love watching TV and have Sky, watch "Sid Roth" or "It's Supernatural" on the Christian Channels. There are many great teachers of the word of God on the Christian channel as well that you can start listening to.

Above all, read your Bible daily and meditate on what you read. Ask the Holy Spirit to give you revelation and understanding in faith, and He will - sometimes immediately, but more often, in His own time. So be patient.

God bless and keep you in Jesus name, amen.